*The Office of Management and Budget
and the Presidency, 1921-1979*

The Office of
Management and Budget
and the Presidency, 1921-1979

Larry Berman

PRINCETON UNIVERSITY PRESS
PRINCETON, NEW JERSEY

For Janet and Scott

CONTENTS

The Office of Management and Budget (OMB) is the most highly developed administrative coordinating and program review unit in the Executive Office of the President (EOP) and offers a unique window for studying the evolution and life style of a public institution. Observers of American politics have long recognized the central role played by OMB through its fiscal and legislative clearance, program coordination and development, budget preparation, and, to a lesser extent, executive management functions.

Recent events, however, have tarnished OMB's image as a once impartial and objective presidential staff agency. During the Watergate period OMB was referred to as The Office of Meddling and Bumbling (TOMB), an appellation characterizing its almost intolerable interference in the internal management processes of departments and agencies. Moreover, by the conclusion of the Nixon administration, all perceptions of OMB's neutrality had been dispelled. President Ford's transition team accused OMB of becoming too involved in departmental policy processes and of uncharacteristically politicizing the budgetary decision-making process. The Congressional Budget Office, House and Senate budget committees, statutory curbs on impoundment, and confirmation requirements for the OMB Director and Deputy Director were intended by Congress as mechanisms for improving OMB's responsiveness to its non-presidential clients. The charges against Bert Lance did nothing to improve the stature of this once proud presidential staff agency.

The perceived politicization of OMB disheartened those who valued OMB's predecessor, the Bureau of the Budget (BOB), as the bastion for "neutral competence" in American government—an American equivalent to the British civil service cadre at Whitehall. In its staff capacity the BOB also faced the danger of overextending its responsibilities into the political and operating levels (the source of OMB's credibility problem) or narrowing its role and viewpoint through concentration on routine details. Nevertheless, between 1921-1970 the BOB lived, at times tenuously, with these occupational hazards and, aside from "green-eyeshade" or "abominable no-man" jokes, escaped public notoriety. If a Budget Director was sometimes used as a presidential fire fighter on pressing political issues, the Budget Bureau as an institution was rarely looked to or perceived as a source of partisan support.

Moreover, an intangible quality separated the old Bureau of the Budget from other Executive Office staff units and from its successor. William Carey characterized it as an institutional pride founded on "the knowledge that [BOB] was indispensable, that it served the presidency to its last ounce of ability, and that it served it well."[1] To those who worked in the old BOB this institutional pride was to be safeguarded at all costs. BOB recruits, educated by the best our civil service offered, emerged from orientation meetings believing that theirs was a select presidential mission. Few spoke in terms of personal pronouns and those seeking individual record building usually found employment elsewhere. Budget Bureau veterans, proud of their relatively small staff size and their location at the center of the resource allocation system in American politics, viewed themselves as the elite of the civil service. BOB officials often told the story that if a Martian army marched on the Capitol, everyone in Washington would flee to the hills, except the Budget Bureau staff, which would stay behind and prepare for an orderly transition in government.

The following chapters offer a mix of history, politics, and personalities in analyzing the evolution of a remarkable institution. The book is also about the institution of the modern presidency and its ability (or lack of it) to cope with ever-increasing programmatic and administrative demands. The narrative is guided by several analytic questions: In a quickly changing environment, can a staff agency at the center of government decision-making adequately meet the President's political needs, the institutional needs of the presidency, and its own organizational requirements? Can OMB be both politically sensitive but not partisan? Why have Presidents utilized OMB for non-institutional purposes? Are there personnel or organizational problems preventing institutional staffs from responding to the demands of activist presidential leadership? What type of staff agency is best suited to helping the President discharge his management responsibilities? What is the optimal relationship within the Executive Office of the President (EOP) between institutional and personal staffs? I seek, therefore, not an exhaustive history of OMB but rather an understanding of why at certain periods in its history, the BOB/OMB performed its staff role differently than at other periods and to what external demands OMB has best responded.

Several years ago Henry Fairlie observed that "the extension of the activities and powers of the Bureau of the Budget is the most obviously unexplored political development in the history of the United States in the past quarter of a century."[2] Moreover, this was so because one of the major obstacles confronting scholars studying the American presidency is lack of accessibility to the subject matter. My data base, however, is primary source information that does make a detailed account possible. The data include unpublished materials from the Records Division of OMB and the Roosevelt through Johnson Presidential Libraries. I have examined thousands of previously unavailable documents such as staff memoranda, self-studies, and personnel evaluations. I have interviewed most former Directors and numerous senior employees who served in the institution from 1939-1978, some with as many as 20-30 years of service.

I have also utilized the results of a questionnaire which I administered to all OMB employees in September 1976 and February 1977. The survey was designed to ascertain OMB personnel's perceptions of possible politicization of OMB during the Nixon presidency, perceptions of OMB's increased involvement in policy-making, perceptions of management improvement efforts since 1970, and the perceived adequacy of OMB as a presidential staff unit.

There is a qualitative change in the archival material between the 1921-1960, 1961-1978 analyses. The 1921-1960 chapters provide an insider's perspective on how the Bureau of the Budget established itself as the central institutional staff support unit within the EOP, and how Budget Bureau Directors and staff sought to maintain that status. The post-1960 analysis then focuses on how external demands, manifesting themselves first in activist presidential leadership and later in the partisan needs of the Nixon administration, undermined BOB's and later OMB's credibility as a presidential agent.

This book was originally submitted as a dissertation to the Department of Politics at Princeton University. The road from thesis to book included intellectual challenge, frustration, bewilderment, and a bit of déjà vu. Several individuals read the final dissertation and offered extensive recommendations for revision. My largest debt is to Professor Fred I. Greenstein of Princeton University, who read more drafts than he or I can remember, and who was a source of unending advice, support and friendship. Professors Hugh Heclo, Richard Neustadt, Robert Rich, Harold Seidman, and Herman Somers provided detailed critiques of the finished dissertation. Elmer Staats, Comptroller General of the United States and a former Budget Bureau official, filled many institutional gaps. Roger Jones, another BOB veteran, read several drafts and provided constant encouragement that such a book should be written.

Mr. Melvin Margerum and his staff at the Records Division of OMB and Elisabeth Knauff, Christine Rudy, and Jennifer Brandt of the OMB Library tracked down many fugitive documents. Ms. Velma Baldwin, OMB's Assistant Director for Administration, cleared the way for my in-house research. I was blessed with a typist of unusual patience and fortitude. Cheryl Lytle of the Davis Political Science Department found her way through a maze of red arrows, scotch tape, and illegible scribbles while finishing the final manuscript.

The book was supported, in part, by grants from the Eleanor Roosevelt Institute, the Harry S Truman Library Institute, the Lyndon Baines Johnson Foundation, the National Science Foundation, and a faculty research grant from the University of California, Davis.

I want to thank my wife, Janet, for her constant support, vitality, and editorial skills. The book is dedicated to Janet and our son Scott.

*The Office of Management and Budget
and the Presidency, 1921-1979*

As with men, institutions have a past which is unalterable and a future which is only dimly perceived. For both, the past must be understood before the forces acting upon them in the future can be forecast with any reasonable chance of success. But only in the present are real choices among alternate courses of action possible.—"The Bureau's Way of Life." Excerpt from a *1959 Self-Study of the Bureau of the Budget.*

A Treasury Bureau or Presidential Staff Agency? 1921-1938

Prior to 1921, federal agencies submitted uncoordinated financial requests directly to the Secretary of the Treasury, where they were packaged with little alteration into a Book of Estimates and forwarded to Congress. The President played only a limited role in formulating the national budget.

By the end of the 19th century, however, federal government expenditures had been increasing rapidly, with twenty-eight years of uninterrupted budget surpluses suddenly followed by six years of deficits between 1904-1910. "It was a foregone conclusion," Louis Fisher noted, "that debt management problems after the war would require modernization of the budget process and an increased financial responsibility for the executive branch."[1]

In 1912 President Taft's Commission on Economy and Efficiency recommended the development of a national executive budget "whereby the executive may be made responsible for getting before the country a definite, well-considered, comprehensive program."[2] The budget reform movement proceeded slowly as World War I, Taft's opposition Congress, and his own re-election defeat removed reform from the immediate agenda. By 1919 Representative James W. Good, Chairman of the House Select Committee on the Budget, introduced a bill placing the President in charge of estimates and assigning Congress responsibility for increasing or reducing those estimates. The Good bill also provided the President with a budgetary agent—a Bureau of the Budget located in the President's office and reporting directly to the Chief Executive. In the Senate, Medill McCormick's

Special Committee on the National Budget also recommended the creation of a Bureau of the Budget. This Senate version, however, located the proposed Bureau in the Treasury Department, not in the President's office.[3]

The House and Senate committees soon compromised by placing the proposed Budget Bureau under presidential control and designating the Secretary of the Treasury as Budget Director. President Wilson vetoed the bill because of a provision that only a concurrent resolution could remove the Comptroller General and Assistant Comptroller General from the General Accounting Office. Concurrent resolutions are not presented to the President for approval and Wilson viewed this as a threat to the Chief Executive's removal powers. The House vote of 198-103 was short of the necessary two-thirds majority to override Wilson's veto. (The 1921 law, which established both the Bureau of the Budget and the General Accounting Office, adopted a joint resolution for removal.)

The impetus for reform could not be stopped. In April 1921, with a new Congress and a new President, the Good and McCormick bills were reintroduced, passed their respective committees, and assigned to conference. By May 25, 1921 a bill emerged calling for the establishment of a Bureau of the Budget, located within the Treasury Department ("in but not of") but headed by a Director and Assistant Director appointed by the President. The Budget Director would be the President's personal assistant, as indicated by the lack of a confirmation requirement. The compromise bill passed both Houses and on June 10, 1921 President Harding signed into law the Budget and Accounting Act.

The Budget and Accounting Act denied federal agencies independent influence in the budget decisions of Congress by specifically empowering the Budget Bureau "to assemble, correlate, revise, reduce, or increase the estimates of the several departments or establishments." The 1921 act also authorized the Budget Bureau to make detailed administrative studies for "secure(ing) greater economy and efficiency in the conduct of the public service."[4] (This particular role in administrative management would be neglected for almost two decades.)

President Harding selected General Charles G. Dawes, a former Chief of Supply Procurement for the American Army in France and a future Vice President of the United States, as the first Director of the Bureau of the Budget. Dawes was an energetic man perfectly suited to the task of bringing the Budget Bureau to life. A BOB Staff Orientation Manual published twenty-five years later acknowledged that "the legislative creation of appropriate budgetary machinery, although a vast advance, could do no more than provide a starting point for the new system. How truly new it would be, how much of a system it would represent, what results it would produce—these were questions unanswerable in statutory terms. Decisive would be the personal leadership in the Bureau of the Budget, the vigor with which it impressed itself upon the departmental structure, and the foresight which it displayed in developing its long-range tasks."[5]

Dawes did not believe the Bureau belonged in the Treasury Department because "the effectiveness of the Budget machinery depends upon its independence of departments and its complete dependence upon the President."[6] In Budget Circular No. 1 of June 29, 1921, Dawes established certain cardinal principles for the Bureau of the Budget. Success of the budget system would depend on basic tenets which needed to be "so firmly established both as concepts and rules of action that they will never hereafter be questioned." These commandments were that the Budget Bureau remain impartial, impersonal, and non-political; the Budget Director act as an advisor to Department officials on matters of business administration; the Director's request for administrative information would take precedence over competing claims of Cabinet officials.

Dawes operated with a definite theory for the role of a nonpolitical presidential managerial staff. While we would now consider the policy-administration dichotomy naive, it

5

reflected the view of the day about organization. Dawes insisted "that the managerial staff to the President had to be completely nonpolitical—they were only workers in the stoke-hole who had nothing to do with the steering of the ship . . . only a nonpolitical staff could do a good managerial job for a political chief executive, and that the best way to let the technicians make their useful professional contribution was to keep them thoroughly subordinated to political authority."[7]

Dawes often insisted that his agency had nothing to do with policy-making and was concerned simply with economy and efficiency in routine government business. "Much as we love the President, if Congress in its omnipotence over appropriations and in accordance with its authority over policy, passed a law that garbage should be put on the White House steps, it would be our regrettable duty, as a bureau, in an impartial, non-political way and non-partisan way to advise the Executive and Congress as to how the largest amount of garbage could be spread in the most expeditious and economical manner."[8] Dawes was, of course, involved in policy-making. The so-called politics-administration dichotomy represented, in practice, not the separation of one from the other, but the dominance of administrative values over political ones.

President Harding gave Dawes great leeway in administrative matters, permitting the Budget Director use of the Cabinet room for scheduling business meetings with Cabinet officers. Harding's visible support allowed the Budget Director to attain the status of primus inter pares. Dawes believed that "no Cabinet officer on the bridge with the President, advising as to what direction the ship of state should sail . . . will properly serve the captain of the ship or its passengers, the public, if he resents the call of the Director of the Budget from the stoke-hole, put there by the captain to see that coal is not wasted."[9] This was a period of retrenchment in government spending. To ensure that coal was not wasted, Dawes established several coordinating agencies headed by a chief coordinator appointed by the President. The agencies dealt with problems of dispersing postwar supplies, organizing departmental purchasing, and preventing wasteful activities. One Bureau report recommended that each employee receive only one pencil at a time and not receive a new one until the unused stub was returned.[10]

Dawes's enthusiasm, his excellent working relationship with the President, and his keen sense of historical mission were important in establishing the Bureau of the Budget as the President's primary staff agent for ensuring economy and efficiency in matters of routine business. Yet, Dawes's insistence that "one cannot successfully preach economy without practicing it," was interpreted as a mandatory self-imposed policy for the Budget Bureau. In the final entry of his diary Dawes wrote that "of the appropriations of $225,000 for the Bureau of the Budget, we only spent $120,313.54 in the year's work. We took our own medicine."[11] Taking its own medicine almost destroyed the usefulness of the Budget Bureau. The emphasis on matters of routine business was countered by Dawes's neglect of government-wide administrative reform. He viewed administrative management as part of the budget review process of identifying waste and reducing spending. The Bureau's *Staff Orientation Manual* noted that "Dawes had not prepared the Bureau for the assumption of functions more typical of a general administrative staff agency. The broader aspects of administrative management, outside the province of economical conduct of business transactions, had not received the attention they deserved."[12]

Dawes's successors, General H. M. Lord and Colonel J. Clawson Roop, showed similar disinterestedness in the broader issues of administrative management. Lord actually checked employees' desks for excessive use of official stationery, paper clips, and other government supplies. Lord engaged in such quaint-sounding ploys as establishing a "Two Per Cent Club" for agency heads who trimmed that amount off their estimates, a "One Per Cent Club" reserved for the less efficient, and the "Loyal Order of Woodpeckers," whose motto read: "All hail to the Loyal Order of Woodpeckers, whose persistent tapping away at waste will make cheerful music in government offices and workshops the coming year." Administrative management activities were reduced to supervising travel regulations and negotiating reduced hotel rates for government employees. The Bureau directed federal agencies to use the Army radio network instead of telephones and gave commendations for taking upper berths in Pullmans and for using brooms until they were completely worn out. Between 1921-1939 the Budget Bureau undertook no organizational studies (despite explicit guidelines of the Budget and Accounting Act.)

A self-imposed parsimony (illustrated by a meager appropriation and staff of forty-five) forced key issues of administrative management to the background. The Bureau consisted of roughly 45 employees. The Bureau's 1921-1938 organization (Appendix Two, A) consisted of the Director's office, two Assistant Directors, an Estimates Division (two or three investigators), clerical assistance, and a General Counsel. The Budget Bureau's own evaluation of the period provides an appropriate epitaph. "The Bureau came to operate increasingly on the basis of settled routines. The indefinite postponement of administrative reorganization and the pride the Bureau took in its diminutive size combined to deprive it of opportunities for significant self-development. . . . At the end of its first decade, the Bureau was no longer able to show effective leadership."[13]

The Budget Bureau initially fared no better under President Roosevelt. Roosevelt's first Budget Director, Lewis Douglas, accepted the BOB Directorship with Roosevelt's assurance that the budget would be balanced. One of Douglas' first tasks was to prepare legislation for reducing federal salaries and veteran's pensions at a combined savings of $500 million. Roosevelt began his first term relying extensively on Douglas. Each morning the Budget Director and Raymond Moley met with the President (in FDR's bedroom) to discuss the important business of the day and, at

8

Roosevelt's request, Douglas attended Cabinet meetings. Ideological differences soon developed between the President and his fiscally conservative Budget Director, primarily over the government's economic policy to combat inflation. Douglas believed that Roosevelt's decision to leave the gold standard was "the end of western civilization."[14] Douglas urged Roosevelt to cut back on New Deal Public Works programs because "history demonstrates, almost without exception, that huge expenditures plunge governments, even though reluctant, into paper inflation. This, history again demonstrates, is one of the most destructive things a government can do to its people."[15] Obviously Roosevelt believed that his New Deal policies were saving people, not destroying them. He questioned Douglas' loyalty and suspected the Budget Director of keeping a secret diary critical of the President's policies. By August 30, 1934 Douglas submitted his resignation to the President, explaining that because temporary measures designed to meet extraordinary conditions had evolved into permanent policy, "in your interests it would be better to replace me with someone who is in more complete accord with your budgetary policies."[16]

The Douglas-Roosevelt split meant that the Bureau's budget work would continue, but the Budget Director would not be an intimate advisor. Wann explains that Roosevelt decided to circumvent the Bureau by devising "other administrative patterns which minimized the role of the Budget Director, and had developed the habit of relying upon personal assistants in the White House to do some of the tasks involved in coordination and administrative management which the Director might have performed better."[17] This decision was reflected in the President's selection of Daniel Bell as Douglas' successor. Bell was a Treasury Department bureaucrat who held a position subordinate to the Secretary of the Treasury, which he refused to surrender in order to maintain his civil service pension. For the next five years Bell served as Acting Director of the Bureau of the Budget.

Yet, between 1932-1936, the Budget Bureau as an insti-

9

tution slowly acquired functions which today still constitute the lifeblood of the American political system. First, as is well documented in Neustadt's work on central clearance, Roosevelt complained at a December 1934 meeting of the National Emergency Council (NEC) about the lack of coordination in agency requests for legislation. All proposals for appropriations would now be cleared by the BOB. All "other" proposed legislation was to go through the Executive Director of the NEC, but with the NEC's demise in 1936 the BOB assumed legislative clearance duties. The new system served Roosevelt's interests. Neustadt observed that "this was Roosevelt's creation, intended to protect not just his budget, but his prerogatives, his freedom of action, and his choice of policies, in an era of fast-growing government and of determined presidential leadership."[18]

In 1938 the Public Printer was persuaded to make multiple copies of enrolled bills so that the Budget Bureau, Congress, and the affected agencies could study proposed legislation *before* it arrived at the White House. The Budget Bureau immediately seized the advantage by issuing Circular 346, officially identifying the BOB as the President's agent on enrolled enactments. Federal agencies were instructed to report within 48 hours their opinions on enrolled enactments, and all agency opinions were to be accompanied by factual information.

The real payoff, however, was that the BOB was able to implement its new veto recommendation authority into the central clearance process. Neustadt describes how "the Budget Bureau's work on agency proposals and reports built up a general, comprehensive record, unmatched elsewhere in government, to buttress its consideration of enrolled bills. At the same time, its mandate on enrolled enactments now lent special point and purpose to clearances of measures in proposed and pending stages."[19]

By 1937, however, President Roosevelt was simply overwhelmed by the administrative aspects of an expanded modern government. The proliferation of New Deal agencies with

10

little regard for administrative patterns, as well as the fact that most of Roosevelt's assistants were assigned to the White House, but on the payroll of other agencies, motivated the President's demand for increased executive control. Roosevelt, believing that expanded government required management tools commensurate to the task, commissioned Louis Brownlow to devise a plan for increased staff support.

On January 10, 1937 President Roosevelt met with his Committee on Administrative Management, several committee staff members, and the majority leaders of the House and Senate to review the Brownlow Committee recommendations. In no uncertain terms, he informed his guests that he needed *both* personal and institutional help.

> The President's task has become impossible for me or any other man. A man in the position will not be able to survive White House service unless it is simplified. I need executive assistants with a "passion for anonymity" to be my legs.
>
> I also need managerial agencies to help me in this job on fiscal, personnel and planning. *Greater aid should be given to me by the Bureau of the Budget,* which now reports to me directly. It should be authorized to improve its staff and to perform certain services on coordination of informational activities.[20]

The "salvation by staff" theme embodied in the Brownlow recommendations was a two-pronged idea: the President would receive both *personal* and *institutional* assistance in the job of being President. These were by no means the same. His personal assistants (few in number) would serve the immediate political interests of the President; the institutional staff (larger in number) would provide continuity and a government-wide perspective of and for the presidency.

The Committee on Administrative Management identified four reasons for the Budget Bureau's failure to develop as an administrative staff agency: (1) inadequate appropriation and personnel shortage; (2) lack of a clear internal organization; (3) anomalous physical location in the Treasury Department; and (4) the restricted view of the Bureau's role held by its Directors.

The Brownlow group argued that it was ludicrous for the Budget Bureau's appropriation to be less than any finance agency or accounting division in government, yet with a staff of 45 be expected to prepare a billion dollar budget. The Budget Bureau's major failing, however, had been in administrative management. Progress had been achieved in the fiscal area, but "at no time has the Bureau of the Budget achieved or even approximated its maximum possible usefulness and effectiveness as an instrument of administrative management."[21] Brownlow looked to the BOB as a directing and controlling agency. The President needed a staff to help manage the executive branch. "The Bureau of the Budget [was] the logical staff agency for the performance of this service. It should be given appropriations and a staff commensurate with the magnitude of the assignment. A relatively small sum invested in strengthening the Bureau of the Budget will yield enormous return in the increased efficiency of Government operation."[22] The Committee also recommended that the Budget Director "be relieved from routine duties and thus enabled to devote himself to problems of fiscal policy and planning."[23]

The BOB *Staff Orientation Manual* uses the subtitle "Rediscovery of Prior Purpose" when describing the 1937 reforms recommended by the Brownlow Committee for upgrading the BOB, noting that "for more than ten years, the original legislative conception of the Budget Bureau as the President's general administrative staff agency remained obscured in the twilight of routine activities."[24] On April 29, 1938 President Roosevelt requested from the House of Representatives a supplemental appropriation of $132,710 for fiscal year 1939. This sum was almost equal to the Bureau's original appropriation of $187,000. The supplement provided for 55 additional employees and various organizational expenses.

On January 12, 1937 Roosevelt forwarded the recommendations of the President's Committee on Administrative Management to Congress. In his message accompanying the Brownlow report, he urged the Congress to understand that "what I am placing before you is not the request for more power, but for the tools of management and the authority to distribute the work so that the President can effectively discharge those powers which the Constitution now places upon him." In spite of Roosevelt's assertion that he sought no increase in power, his reorganization plan met with vociferous opposition in Congress, with the opposition expressing fear of executive dictatorship. The Reorganization Bill originally submitted to Congress was defeated.[25] After much political negotiating, however, the basic lines of the Brownlow report were enacted into law in Reorganization Plan 1 of April 25, 1939,[26] which established the new Executive Office of the President (EOP) and transferred to it the Bureau of the Budget (from Treasury) and the National Resources Planning Board (from Interior).

The reinvigorated Bureau of the Budget (BOB) was at the center of this newly institutionalized Presidency. The functions assigned to the Budget Bureau by Executive Order 8248 of September 8, 1939 illustrate the magnitude of the Budget Bureau's role. In fact, the group of management consultants responsible for drafting the Executive Order soon constituted the core of the BOB staff. Bernard Gladieux, Joseph Pois, Larry Hoelscher, Arnold Miles, and Elmer Staats shared backgrounds with the Public Administration Service in Chicago and were interested in seeing that the BOB played a leading and vital part in improving the organization and management of the Federal government. The Executive Order provided the Budget Bureau with authority to:

1. Assist the President in the preparation of the Budget and the formulation of the fiscal program of the Government.
2. Supervise and control the administration of the Budget.
3. Conduct research in the development of improved plans of administrative management, and to advise the executive departments and agencies of the Government with re-

13

    spect to improved administrative organization and practice.

4. Aid the President to bring about more efficient and economical conduct of Government service.

5. Assist the President by clearing and coordinating departmental advice on proposed legislation and by making recommendations as to Presidential action on legislative enactments, in accordance with past practice.

6. Assist in the consideration and clearance and, where necessary, in the preparation of proposed Executive orders and proclamations, in accordance with the provisions of Executive Order 7289 of February 18, 1936.

7. Plan and promote the improvement, development, and coordination of Federal and other statistical services.

8. Keep the President informed of the progress of activities by agencies of the Government with respect to work proposed, work actually initiated, and work completed, together with the relative timing of work between the several agencies of the Government; all to the end that the work programs of the several agencies of the Executive Branch of the Government may be coordinated and that the monies appropriated by the Congress may be expended in the most economical manner possible with the least possible overlapping and duplication of effort.

The born-again Budget Bureau needed leadership of far greater vision and administrative ability than it had received since 1921. On March 11, 1939 Harold D. Smith, Budget Director for the state of Michigan, was appointed by President Roosevelt as Director of the reconstituted Bureau of the Budget. Both a strong proponent of the Brownlow recommendations for administrative reform and a personal friend of Brownlow, Smith molded the Budget Bureau into an indispensable presidential managerial staff and, in doing so, established the Budget Director as a key advisor to the President. Smith possessed a far broader vision of the BOB's role in the federal system than his predecessors and is truly one of the unheralded administrators in the history of American political institutions. During his tenure, the Bureau staff increased to over 600. Of additional import is that many of the people Smith recruited remained in the Bureau for the next two decades and in some cases became the leading civil servants in the expanded modern government. The following chapter illustrates the Budget Bureau's emergence as primus inter pares in the executive office as a combination of both Smith's extraordinary personal relationship with Roosevelt and the *need* for central coordination in a vastly expanded, activist federal government.

The Development of an Institutional
Bureau of the Budget, 1939-1952

"I would like to say, too—what I fear can never be said adequately—that I am proud of the team which is the staff of the Bureau of the Budget; that in our tasks we have unusual opportunities for real accomplishment; that the more we work as a team, the better able we will be to grasp those opportunities. All of us, I think, feel personal satisfaction in belonging to this team."—Harold Smith, Preface to *BOB Staff Orientation Manual,* 1945.

"Your three years of service as Director of the Budget may not have added to your life expectancy, but I can assure you that your faithful work has increased mine."—President Roosevelt to Harold Smith, April 21, 1942.

How did Harold Smith establish his BOB as the institutional fulcrum within the EOP? How did the Bureau of the Budget in 1939 with a new location and increased appropriation make itself useful to the President? Smith began on May 18, 1939 by notifying all Bureau personnel that he was "anxious to give thought and attention to any matters which may be concerned with our organization and its work. Especially do I think this important in view of possible new or increased responsibilities in connection with the general reorganization plans."[1] He suggested that each member of the staff "dictate any reflections he may have concerning his own job or the overall conception of the Bureau and its program of work. No detail should be considered too small to receive attention." By the next day several frank evaluations of the "old" and recommendations for the "new" Budget Bureau filtered to the Director's office, all bearing the authors' signature.

16

Smith's opinion poll set a precedent and delighted the staff. As one individual wrote, "your invitation to express our views along any line we choose, sets a precedent and I hope produces ideas that will be so helpful to all concerned, that the policy will be continued and that we may feel free to contact you personally or by letter and present our views for consideration."[2]

Bureau personnel, sensing the advent of a new era, provided Smith with an extensive list of personnel and equipment requests. Recommendations included improved indirect lighting for facilitating night work, the appointment of a drafting attorney, creation of a budget liaison office, additional personnel with estimates experience, stenographic personnel, dictaphones, a telephone service, new typists, filing cabinets, and development of an internal personnel policy. One bold staffer recommended that the Bureau's appropriation for supplies be increased and attached a chart showing the Bureau's purchasing of all office equipment since 1921. Incredible as it may seem, the chart disclosed that the Bureau owned only one adding machine, one calculating machine, and one bookkeeping manual—all purchased in 1921.[3]

BOB staff recommendations pertaining to the relationship between themselves and the President's new Secretaries are especially interesting. Executive Order 8248 assigned Secretaries to the President for facilitating and maintaining communication with the Congress, the heads of executive departments and agencies, the press, the radio, and the general public. Budget staff wanted clear lines of communication between the BOB and presidential staff, despite Roosevelt's propensity to cross them. One BOB staffer recommended that the new Secretaries actually be given offices within the BOB in order to guarantee better coordination. Smith disagreed with this recommendation and in the published digest[4] changed "within" to "near." The same staffer wrote that "instead of the somewhat 'hit or miss' system now in effect whereby the Budget Director discusses matters with the President as emergencies arise, it would be more satisfactory if a certain time could be set aside for that purpose each week, supplemented by other contacts in case of emergencies."[5] Smith agreed totally with this recommendation but "hit or miss" was a strong way of expressing it. Subsequently, in the official digest Smith replaced "hit or miss" with "intermittently" and called for a "definite schedule of conferences for clearing on problems of legislation and administrative organization, supplemented by other contacts in case of emergencies."

BOB staffers were also concerned that clear jurisdictional responsibility be established between themselves and the more personal-political White House staff. As one individual expressed it, "the White House staff frequently makes recommendations to the President contrary to those made by the Bureau of the Budget. Some method should be provided to clear recommendations with this staff in order that conflicting recommendations will not be made."[6] By protecting its turf, the Bureau was attempting to establish itself as the one point in government where the President could get a government-wide perspective. Lack of coordination placed a burden upon the President and often created embarrassing situations. For example, a typical administrative problem occurred in 1939 when the Bureau formulated a plan for reducing the Civil Conservation Corps (CCC) to 1,250. President Roosevelt approved the plan and the CCC was notified of the reduction. Nevertheless, CCC officials contacted the White House staff and later informed the BOB that they had been advised by the White House that the President had not intended to make the CCC reduction. On another occasion the White House staff approved a plan for releasing all Coast Guard Warrant Officers, contrary to a plan presented by BOB and approved by the President.[7]

Several staffers argued that the President often made decisions on the basis of inadequate information, when this information could be provided by the BOB staff. The official digest noted that, "the President should be impressed with the importance of deferring decisions on matters presented by various Cabinet Officers and representatives of agencies until referred to the Budget Bureau."[8] One staff person discussed this short-circuiting of the Bureau. "If the President would agree to submit to the Director all matters taken up with him, which would or might lead to drafts upon the Treasury, before he commits himself, I am satisfied the BOB could render him and the government valuable service."[9]

These staff responses reflect an intent (an institutional need perhaps), to transcend the restricted role played by the pre-1939 Budget Bureau. The emphasis on protecting the President's options and providing an impartial analysis not otherwise available from the Cabinet or White House assistants revealed a perception among Bureau staff that they could provide key staff services to the President. For the Bureau to play such a role, however, an organizational structure would be required which supported both the staff's government-wide perspective and the Director's more personal relationship with Roosevelt (as recommended by Brownlow).

In 1940 Director Smith established five divisions in the Budget Bureau. These divisions (Appendix Two, B) provided horizontal coordination on all issues that entered the Budget Bureau and ensured the Director five separate analyses based on each division's functional perspective. This organizational balance was supported by certain general principles. Five separate functional divisions staffed with specialists and organized from a government-wide perspective would avoid one narrow viewpoint. These separate viewpoints could be synthesized into a workable solution with all unresolved issues determined by the Director. Career division chiefs would advise the Director in their areas of specialization while overseeing their respective staffs. The Director would not be encumbered with a large staff, thereby allowing flexibility for interacting with the President.

Estimates, the largest division, had responsibility for formulating and presenting the President's budget to Congress. Division staff were organized on a clientele basis with the agencies and continually reviewed agency and departmental budget requests. The Fiscal Division advised the Estimates Division on matters of budget detail and assisted the Director on matters of general fiscal policy. Director Smith staffed this division with some of the country's leading economists. Legislative Reference assisted in the coordination and clearance of proposed legislation, enrolled bills, executive orders, and proclamations. Administrative Management was responsible for studies in organization and management improvement in government departments and agencies. Statistical Standards assisted in the promotion of improving statistical information and standardizing report collecting.

Smith's most difficult job came in filling these organizational boxes. The recruitment problem occupied most of his time during his first year and a half in office. After only a few months as Budget Director, he recorded in his diary, "I have impressed everyone in the top staff of the Bureau with the necessity of very careful examination of each person taken on the staff of the Bureau, in order that we may make a minimum of errors. Nothing is so important to us as 'able personnel.' "[10] In another entry Smith observed that, "it has been my desire to go over each appointment in the Bureau with a fine tooth comb in order that few mistakes may be made in adding to the staff."[11]

For Smith, the recruitment issue was often one of quality, not quantity. "The matter of interviewing personnel is occupying a good deal of my time. The BOB has some 50 vacant positions including those authorized for next year, and we are having the devil's own time in securing persons with sufficiently broad background and experience, who at the same time have balanced outlook and judgement concerning governmental problems. . . . More and more I am impressed with the value of broad training in the social sciences and the development of people with planning types of minds."[12] Smith placed a premium on individuals who valued the good of the organization over their personal goals. He wrote in his diary that when confronted with a problem far too many people thought "in terms of the individual rather than in terms of organization . . . the individuals come and go but the organization remains. The staff of the Executive Office of the President least of all can afford to think in terms solely of individuals. More trouble is developed, more things gone awry in the Federal Government to my knowledge because of this tendency."[13]

Smith's concern for recruiting the "right" person for a key job is illustrated by his pursuit of economists J. Weldon Jones, Gardiner Means, Paul David, and Gerhard Colm for the Bureau's Fiscal Division. Smith envisioned the Fiscal Division developing into the President's primary staff for substantive economic policy. The dream ended with the creation of the Council of Economic Advisors in 1946 and in 1952 the Fiscal Division was abolished. A Fiscal Section remained as part of the Budget Review Division. Smith spent eleven months convincing J. Weldon Jones, Financial Advisor to the U.S. High Commissioner to the Philippines, in Manila, to return from overseas and head the new Fiscal Division.

On October 20, 1939 (Jones would be sworn in almost a year later on November 22, 1940) Smith wrote to Jones in the Philippines on the subject of heading the Bureau's Fiscal Division. The Director explained that the Budget Bureau was now part of the President's Executive Office with greater expanded responsibilities and that "you may have that combination of administrative background, knowledge of accounting and appreciation of the broader economic implications of fiscal problems that would fit the conception we have for this position."[14]

When Jones declined, Smith persuaded a mutual friend, Edward Kemp, to appeal to Jones. Kemp took the angle that the new Budget Bureau offered vastly expanded opportunities to help the President.

> Consider the Budget Office as no longer a minor adjunct of the Treasury but as a chief arm of the executive, next to the throne, so to speak. It will steadily grow in importance and rank. Dividing the functions of the budget office into five units, in the fiscal division which you would head as an As-

> sistant Director, will be placed the responsibility for supervising the fiscal operations of the government departments under their budget allotments. . . . It may well become the key position in the government with respect to fiscal policy. . . .[15]

Jones again declined the offer (it is possible that High Commissioner Sayre prevented him from taking the position) and the matter appeared settled. A few months later, however, Wayne Coy (later Smith's Assistant Director) wrote to Jones that he and Smith would accept "no answer from you except 'yes.'" Coy also described the new BOB as "undergoing a change of function at the present time . . . assuming a far more important role than it has ever occupied heretofore. In addition to its traditional function of budget making, it is beginning to function as an administrative management agency, thereby becoming a vital part of the day-to-day operation of the entire government. Secondly, the changing concept of the function of this office gives it a role in the determination of the fiscal policy of the government."[16]

A short time thereafter Jones accepted the job as head of the Fiscal Division. The correspondence illustrates Smith's relentless pursuit of the right person for a key BOB job. Director Smith and his allies now had a product to sell—the modern Bureau of the Budget.

Smith was determined that his staff's product not be duplicated anywhere in the federal service. Subsequently, under his active encouragement, BOB staffers were indoctrinated with the philosophy that they served the President and the presidency. Smith saw himself as the Director of an institutional career staff, distinct from personal White House aides, but concerned with the problems of the President and the institution of the presidency. Neustadt noted that Smith "tried to build and operate his Bureau accordingly, not as a 'budget' staff but as a presidential staff which was organized around the budget process for the sake both of convenience and opportunity."[17]

22

Smith synthesized his role as presidential personal advisor with his institutional responsibilities as Budget Director. As a professional public administrator, he understood the potential dangers for the institution if the Director neglected his household responsibilities. (In fact, a staff paper prepared for a BOB self-study almost three decades later argued that many Bureau staffers "regard Harold Smith as the last Director who paid adequate attention to management and organization.") While Roosevelt looked to Smith for personal, ad hoc assistance, the President usually distinguished institutional from personal-partisan assignments. Stephen Hess observed that, "Roosevelt was relatively meticulous in using the Bureau of the Budget for institutional purposes."[18] Harold Seidman cites the example of Roosevelt's instructing his administrative assistant, James Rowe, to assist in the enrolled bill process, but "his job was to look after the President, and the Budget Bureau's to protect the interests of the Presidency."[19] Paul Appleby noted that Roosevelt, "always felt (the Budget Bureau) was a good place to refer things; there he would get a workmanlike job done; there not much would be overlooked; there no important 'boner' would be committed; there the whole Government would be considered. Only when political considerations were pronounced and when urgency seemed to dictate sweeping action rather than initial craftsmanship was the reference likely to be made elsewhere."[20]

This distinction between the President's personal and institutional interests represents the cornerstone of the BOB's success between 1939 and 1945. Some readers may regard this personal-institutional distinction as elementary to Executive branch organization. The future tendency of Presidents and Directors to blur or ignore the distinction, however, eventually created role dilemmas for the BOB, and deprived the President of a desperately needed perspective. Harold Smith understood what some of his successors did not—that the political interests of the President and the long-term

23

interests of the presidency as an institution are not the same, and that if a President happens to ignore this distinction, a Budget Director should be around to remind him of it.

Smith also understood that Roosevelt needed someone to be his S.O.B. if such a capacity protected the President from those who would undercut his authority. Smith's ticket into Roosevelt's advisory circle was the Budget Director's ability to offer the President something that most of his other aides could not—objective, impartial advice based on the BOB's staff work. In 1943, for example, a problem arose in surplus property and Smith believed its cause was careless administration in the White House and the Office of War Mobilization (OWM). He recorded in his diary that he "was greatly distressed over the question of what the Bureau of the Budget is to do in connection with the surplus property and what Justice Byrnes and OWM are to do." He thought the situation contained the seeds of "scandal" and offered to "tackle the President if [White House Special Counsel Samuel] Rosenman thought it would do any good. I was perfectly willing to be a S.O.B. if it meant any protection to him."[21] If there was one quality which Smith displayed over all others, it was his genuine concern for protecting the President's options from individuals who threatened them. Roosevelt, on the other hand, rarely committed himself to a policy line before hearing from several advisory channels. At first Smith was but one of several checkpoints on whom FDR relied and the Budget Director did not escape Roosevelt's habit of playing advisors against one another. But Smith, with a growing staff component, possessed unparalleled information resources and before long Roosevelt turned more and more to his "Mr. Fix-it." From Smith, the President needed three services. "*First*, he wanted cool, detached appraisals of the financial, managerial, *and* program rationality in departmental budget plans and legislative programs. *Second*, he wanted comparable appraisals of the bright ideas originating in his own mind, or the minds of his political and personal associates. *Third*, he wanted the White House backstopped by preliminary and subsidiary staff work of the sort his own aides could not undertake without forfeiting their availability and flexibility as a small group of generalists on his immediate business."[22]

The Roosevelt-Smith relationship took many forms. During Smith's first weeks in office, the Budget Director advised Roosevelt in matters dealing with administrative overhead allowances on WPA projects, a federal office decentralization program, a liaison between War, State, and Interior Departments on territorial government, office space in the EOP, and appointment of agency administrators. Smith described this last assignment as, "the first hot one the President has handed me." Roosevelt had asked Smith and Press Secretary Steve Early to straighten out a problem between the Civil Service Commission and the War Department. Smith noted that "this problem has nothing to do with budgeting [however] it looks as if the President might be trying me out on this one, which [is] pretty hot. . . ."[23]

When Smith learned of organizational problems in the new Wages and Hours Division of the Labor Department, he wrote that "unless the situation improves I shall take the matter to the President, since knowing about it, I feel an obligation to report."[24] A few days later he went to the President and received instructions to do whatever necessary for properly organizing Wages and Hours. Smith realized that this was "an opportunity for the Budget Office to demonstrate in practical terms what it means to render assistance to the President in matters of management."[25]

During another meeting Smith recommended an increase of 10 percent in existing taxes. "I briefly indicated that I thought there might be a more constructive approach, and that in the absence of such an approach that somebody would likely introduce from the opposition an excess profits tax. I wanted to put the President on his guard."[26] Roosevelt's trust in Smith is illustrated from Smith's April 12, 1941 dairy notes: "The President told me of the plans he was developing unannounced for patrolling the Atlantic. He told me these plans very confidentially. Only four members of the Cabinet knew about them, and the President doubted that he would tell the others because they could not keep their mouths shut."[27]

Smith's dedication to the institution of the presidency is evident in the Budget Director's efforts to ameliorate organizational problems in the War Manpower Commission. Roosevelt was so annoyed with the Commission's administrative blunders that he was prepared to fire its chairman, Paul McNutt. On November 23, 1942 Smith sent Roosevelt a memorandum on the organizational problems in the War Manpower Commission, which Roosevelt later described as "the best he had received during his whole administration."[28]

Smith informed Roosevelt that the President was unfairly blaming McNutt for the Commission's problems, and that firing the chairman could do more harm than good. He prefaced his recommendations by reminding Roosevelt, "I feel that I would not be fair to you as Chief Executive or to my own conscience if I did not set forth rather fully and completely what I know and think about the current manpower situation. I believe that I have something to contribute in a somewhat different vein and plane than the information already available to you from other sources. . . . *I am not conscious of any factors which would distort my objectivity.*"[29]

Smith argued that the real problem resided in the administrative setup under McNutt, and that this "had done much to put McNutt in a bad light." He assured Roosevelt that he was not "making an argument for McNutt on any personal basis," but the real issue was that of a bad staff ruining a good man. He informed Roosevelt that the Budget Director and McNutt had discussed the problem and McNutt would revamp administrative operations in the Manpower Commission. Two weeks later Roosevelt informed Smith that the memorandum had converted the President, Harry Hopkins, and James Byrnes.

Nothing delighted the Budget Director more than Roosevelt's acknowledgment of the Budget staff's contribution. On December 30, 1939, following an all-day budget meeting with the President before submitting the budget to Congress, Roosevelt "suggested that I should take a vacation while Congress was getting under way and that I should arrange to run if possible the Budget on a skeleton staff so that other staff members who had worked day and night for the last several months could get some chance of recuperation. He generally seems quite pleased with the Budget job, and with the Budget message."[30] Recuperation was exactly what some staff members néeded. On January 16, 1940 Smith noted in his diary the poor health of a Mr. Robinson, head of the BOB's service section. "There is nothing organically wrong with him, simply overwork. I kidded him by saying that I really didn't want to get the reputation of killing people on the job. A good many uninformed persons talk about pay-rollers but few people realize how many public servants break their health by overwork and nervous strain on the job."[31] Smith took a short vacation, but returned early to attend a White House reception for Department officials in mid-January: "When [I] shook hands with the President he again expressed surprise in seeing me, thinking that I was on vacation and wondered why I had come back so soon. I told him that there were too many problems around here to leave, and Mrs. Smith told him that I had run out of money."[32] Smith, in fact, frequently joked about his dedication. During a rare day off he played some golf and later read Willoughby's *The National Budget*. Smith's August 11, 1939 diary entry read, "my vacation is a good deal like the cab driver, who takes a ride on his day off."[33] One can understand Roosevelt's reaction upon receiving Smith's pro forma resignation following the President's 1944 election victory: "I would no more accept your resignation than fly by jumping off a roof. You are essentially personna grata and doing a fine job. [Your idea] is bum."[34]

Less than one hundred days after the Bureau's transfer to the EOP, Germany invaded Poland. Between 1940 and 1943 the Budget Bureau constituted the sole staff support for the President in managing the defense and, later, the war effort. The role of the BOB during this wartime period illustrates the more positive role which OMB could take with respect to organization and management of the executive branch. The Bureau of the Budget immediately shifted its resources to helping the President in preparing and managing the war effort. The Bureau's Division of Administrative Management was assigned responsibility for coordinating the administrative problems of the war and the alphabet agencies. The expansion of Bureau responsibilities was reflected in the increase in Administrative Management personnel from 37 in 1940 to 77 by June 1942. Former BOB official Roger Jones recalled that, "the Bureau had to concern itself with kinds of problems which it had not expected to take on. The organization of the defense program, the rearrangement of the budget to give a higher priority to defense matters, the realignment of national priorities and national resources against the possibility that the European War would make demands that were not in our thinking at all. . . . There was rapid acceleration of attention to the Budget Bureau's role as an organization and management planner for the President and as a sorter out of fiscal priorities and possibilities."[35]

In 1941, $100,000 was allocated from the President's emergency fund for the establishment of a special defense unit within the Budget Bureau. The war unit collected information on defense expenditures by field examinations, assured that the inspection work carried on by the defense agencies was properly organized, and guaranteed that the Bureau be informed on the effects of defense expenditures on non-defense activities.

Between 1941 and 1944 the BOB's Defense Projects Unit expanded from 12 to 61. This unit focused on referrals from the President and included analyzing problems in defense labor supply administration, planning for field offices for the Office of Emergency Management, studying the field organization and management of the Office of Production Management, and organizing the staff of the Board of Economic Welfare.

The BOB discharged three major war-related activities.[36] First, the Bureau helped in planning the organization of the country's war program, particularly in setting up war agencies and establishing the scope of their responsibilities. The War Manpower Commission, the Office of War Information, the Office of Emergency Management, the Office of Price Administration, and the Office of Economic Stabilization all came into existence as a result of BOB staff work. Second, the Bureau conducted studies aimed at improving government business management for wartime needs. Third, the Bureau assisted federal agencies in their internal administrative problems.

Included among the Bureau's new statutory responsibilities were classifying federal agencies according to their relative importance to the war effort in order to expedite personnel transfers to key agencies; coordinating and improving surveying and mapping activities in federal agencies; publishing government statistics, insuring compliance with established policy and wartime interests of the United States; establishing control over the distribution and utilization of supplies and equipment of federal agencies; making quarterly determinations of the number of employees needed in federal agencies for efficient exercise of their responsibilities; reviewing agency plans for public works; reporting consolidated programs to the President; clearing agency reports on proposed public works projects as to their relationship to the President's program; and preparing recommendations for the liquidation of war agencies.

During the war several competitors threatened the Bureau's newly acquired status as primus inter pares in the EOP. The Office of War Mobilization (OWM) eventually assumed responsibility for most high priority policy planning functions. The BOB was, in theory, concerned with structure, financing, and organizational coordination among agencies, whereas OWM focused on substantive guidance and advice to the President and on the relationship of the civilian side of the war program to the military side. Obviously, there was plenty of room for differences of opinion on specific issues. Herman Somers noted that "there was a growing tendency to disregard the Bureau and to act independently except for direct approval or disapproval of the President."[37] Smith clashed with OWM Director Byrnes on jurisdictional responsibilities because Smith believed OWM "was an unnecessary agency duplicating many of the Bureau's functions, without the Bureau's facilities for carrying them out."[38] Nevertheless an amicable relationship developed between OWM and BOB staff, with each curious of the other and unsure of its own post-World War responsibilities.

On January 4, 1945 Director Smith conferred with Roosevelt on the President's forthcoming Budget Message. Smith recorded in his diary how tired Roosevelt looked, "his cigarette holder did not seem to have its usual jaunty tilt . . . he seemed a little more stooped than usual . . . he appeared as a man who, while in possession of his very great faculties, seemed tired in using them." Smith concluded his entry with a resolution that "I would do my best not to trouble the President with anything ordinary or petty and that I would do everything possible to relieve him of every burden of administration that the Bureau of the Budget could conceivably handle. I will choke off staff memorandums to the President prepared for my signature and I will in other ways do my best to relieve him of any burden that I can. This perhaps is the closest I have come to making a New Year's resolution."[39]

By April 12, 1945, however, President Franklin D. Roosevelt died from a massive cerebral hemorrhage while vacationing in Warm Springs, Georgia. The following day Harold Smith wrote President Truman pledging "my support in any way in which you may wish me to serve."[40] Smith added that "few men have been in a better position than I to appreciate the heavy responsibilities and onerous burdens of the Presidency." In a memorandum to Bureau staff, Smith observed that Roosevelt's reliance on the Budget Bureau and "our close appreciation of him makes our sorrow the deeper with his passing."[41] But he reminded his staff that the BOB served the presidency as well as the President. "The tasks that were dropped remain to be completed. . . . We must now turn the best of our abilities and our energies to performing the tasks required of us by our new President." The Bureau's efforts in helping President Truman began the same day, when Bureau staff analyzed Truman's actions as Senator so that the BOB could be prepared to act consistently with the new President's thinking.

Six days following Roosevelt's death, Smith had his first conference with the President. He recorded that when he entered the President's office Truman was standing by the window. "This was a contrast to seeing President Roosevelt, who could not move from his chair. . . . President Truman greeted me cordially and said, "That was a nice letter you sent me." Truman informed Smith that he wanted the Budget Director to stay. "You have done a good job as Director of the Bureau. . . . I have a tremendous responsibility and I want you to help me. If I ever want a new Budget Director you'll be the first to know about it. That's the way I do business."[42]

Smith thanked the President for his confidence and indicated that Truman "should feel no obligation whatsoever to me personally." Smith added that he had enjoyed "a close personal relationship with President Roosevelt, which I felt had a considerable bearing upon the status of the Bureau of the Budget and the Government's business in general."[43]

Smith's first task was to educate Truman on the various aspects of the BOB's job. Truman and his incoming staff tended to view the BOB's role in budgetary terms. Neustadt quotes John Snyder's perspective that "I simply do not see why *policy* is any business of the Budget Bureau,"[44] as a view shared by Truman. Smith informed the President that Roosevelt had utilized the Budget Director in all kinds of policy matters, but Truman was under no obligation to follow Roosevelt's precedent. At their first meeting Smith described the dichotomies of the Budget Director's role.

> When I mentioned the fact that he should be aware that the Director of the Budget was always bringing up problems, President Truman said that he liked problems so I need not worry on that score. I told him how I had once remarked to President Roosevelt that I would not blame him if he never saw me again, for I was in the unhappy position of constantly presenting difficulties. I had said, "Secretary Ickes can come in here and report, 'Mr. President, Grand Coulee Dam has just been completed. It is a great engineering feat. The people of the area are delighted. This will have a good influence on the whole economy of the Northwest.' But the Director of the Budget has to come in and say, 'I'm sorry, Mr. President, but the foundations of Grand Coulee Dam are faulty.' " President Truman laughed and said he understood the kind of role that I had to play.[45]

During their second meeting, Smith explained the breadth of his agency's institutional staff work.

> I pointed out that often we undertake studies on our own initiative or upon the suggestion of some Department without bothering the President; that sometimes when we are fairly well along someone dashes into the President's office with an ex parte presentation; that this kind of thing causes a good deal of trouble in the government and upsets our efforts. The President said emphatically that he does not propose to accept any ex parte presentation; that I need not worry on this score; that anything that falls within our purview will be kicked back to us; and that he does not intend to sign Executive Orders without careful clearance. I indicated that I appreciated very much his attitude. I said to the President that if I ever failed to give him all the facts and both sides of the story that failure would be due *only* to my ignorance of a situation and not any intent on my part. I have always tried to give the Chief Executive all of the facts.[46]

32

Afterwards Smith wrote: "The whole conference was highly satisfactory from my point of view. It revealed to me that the President is actually accepting me as Director of the Budget and that much of my worry about the possibility that I would stand in the way of the development of the Bureau of the Budget as an institution was allayed. The President's reactions were positive and highly intelligent. While he agreed with nearly all of our propositions, I did not feel that I was selling him a bill of goods."[47] There was, however, uncertainty about the role of the BOB for a few months following Roosevelt's death. Smith reported almost nothing to the BOB staff about his early rapport with the President. The Budget Director was a little uncertain how his relationship would develop and he was concerned about the role of the Office of War Mobilization and Reconversion [OWMR] (which had been moving positively and with not much tact for Budget Bureau functions).[48]

Truman believed in broader delegations of authority to his Cabinet officers than Roosevelt had, and he developed an advisory process in which policies came to him not for development but instead for decision. The basis of Truman's operating style was to gather all the facts possible, and to make a decision based on those facts. Smith noticed almost immediately Truman's desire to "establish departmental lines so clearly that he will be able to put his finger on the responsible person."[49] Former BOB official Roger Jones believed that this type of administrative operation posed a problem for Smith because "the assignments from Roosevelt had always been such that Smith was free to go in any way or direction he wanted to, whereas under Mr. Truman there was always a direct line of—you come directly back to me."[50] In dealing with his Budget Director, Truman was straightforward and expected the facts. Smith noted that "at one point in my discussion with the President I rather apologized for attacking him so vigorously on these various subjects. The President said most cordially, 'you can talk to me about anything. I want to know the facts.' This pleased me very much because one of the marks of an able executive is willingness to hear all points of view and refuse to shut off all the channels of information."[51]

President Truman used the Budget Bureau as his personal institutional staff arm in managing the federal government, viewing the BOB as the key component in an institutional presidency. Richard Rose noted that Truman "expected the Bureau of the Budget to do the staff work for him as career officials in the Executive Office, while he himself made the decisions that were constitutionally and politically the responsibility of the President."[52] While taping his Oral History for deposit in the Truman Library, Roger Jones was asked if, because he was a registered Republican, President Truman ever requested his assistance in the 1948 presidential campaign. Jones responded: "NO. NO. NO. Mr. Truman would not have asked anybody in the Budget Bureau, including the Director, to work in that kind of way. He wanted this place to be institutional, and we were."[53]

However, all was not smooth sailing for the Budget Director. On October 30, 1945 Smith informed Truman that the President was not getting maximum production from BOB staff because practically no one in the White House understood Bureau responsibilities. Smith referred to a proposed stabilization order that arrived at the Bureau too late for close scrutiny by the Office of Legislative Reference. The Director said that this was not a bureaucratic protest, but "the result of a desire to express to you my feeling that unless all of us serving you have an opportunity to do better staff work, we will generate trouble for you rather than keep your troubles at a minimum as I believe we should always strive to do."[54]

During a May 5, 1945 meeting with Truman, Smith "indicated that I have a habit of being frank and that if the President wanted to knock my ears down on any subject he should do so. He replied, 'I like frankness.' *The President's words and manners indicated he greatly appreciated my effort to protect him.*"[55] The President quickly learned that a Cabinet

34

officer was a party of interest in many policy issues. In 1945 the Department of Labor was reorganized and several administrators maneuvered for jurisdiction over the United States Employment Service. Smith informed Truman that "this was the kind of decision which the President would have to make; that he could not rely solely on the advice of his Cabinet members in such matters simply because it was in the nature of things that they would become advocates."[56] In January 1946 Truman asked his Budget Director why it was that once a person was appointed to the Cabinet he became so touchy and difficult to deal with. Truman told Smith, "what a time I am having with some of my prima donnas. I simply don't understand it. More and more I am beginning to see what President Roosevelt put up with. Can you tell me why it is that men whom I have known for some time and with whom I have been accustomed to deal have now become so touchy. Is there something that the President always does wrong?"[57] Smith responded that he "had observed that those working close to the President always developed certain jealousies and a certain touchiness which was almost akin to an occupational disease. I said I was conscious of some of the factors in this picture because I had had to make some applications to myself; but perhaps because I had no ambitions, I had not become too much involved and had remained in a fairly objective position for observing others." The President remarked, "You have been interested in doing a job. That's the difference."

On March 7, 1946 Secretary of State Byrnes asked Smith to consider being the United States candidate for Assistant Secretary General of the United Nations. Smith was very interested in the job. When Byrnes called President Truman on this issue (with whom he had not previously checked), the President said, "My God, you can't take that fellow." When Byrnes informed Truman that Smith would soon be leaving the Bureau because of financial problems, the President "apparently said that he could better afford to lose me in a year or so than he could now."[58]

On June 19, 1946 (14 months after Roosevelt's death), Harold Smith submitted his resignation as Director of the Bureau of the Budget so that he could accept the Vice-Presidency of the International Bank for Reconstruction and Development. In his letter of resignation Smith commented on his seven years service for two Presidents. "I have enjoyed my work in the Bureau of the Budget. In particular, I have felt a sense of satisfaction about having had your tolerant and sympathetic support at all times. This has meant a great deal to me personally, and I know that it has meant much to the Bureau as an institution in Federal administration. I shall always cherish as a pleasant memory your warm support of the Bureau and of myself."[59]

Smith explained that he was leaving the Budget Bureau because of "the prospect of assisting in the promotion of world prosperity and peace," and "because it offers greater compensation."[60] Smith's annual salary as Budget Director was $10,000. He would receive $22,500 tax free in his new job.

President Truman, in accepting Smith's resignation, noted that "besides great ability, you brought to the work fidelity, integrity and loyalty. I know, too, at what great financial sacrifice you have served your government. This is too often a tragedy of public service. I can only say: well done, and tender you the thanks of the nation which you have served with such unselfish devotion."[61]

Thus ended the longest Budget directorship in the history of the BOB/OMB. (There have been nine Directors in the last decade.) Smith's most important contribution came in establishing the Bureau as the institutional heart of the EOP. Neustadt observed that Smith "equipped himself to be an institutional chief-of-staff for the President, receiving separate inputs that incorporated different viewpoints, so his focus and his tasks of recommendations would be somewhat like the President, except in respect of the purely personal and the party political, these Smith regarded as domains for 'personal' staff."[62]

Every Budget Director has the important responsibility of educating the President on the role of the BOB/OMB, that is, what he can expect from the agency and what he cannot. The Director has to communicate to the President that the BOB/OMB is different from a President's personal staff. In addition, the Director needs to be seen by his staff as a person who understands the music they march to. The Director is the President's aide, but he is also the bridge to the President for those working for the presidency. Smith succeeded admirably on all counts. Even when acting as Roosevelt's "Mr. Fix-it," he tried to protect his Bureau's institutional perspective. As administrative problems arose, Roosevelt often asked Smith to take care of it personally, and not use his Bureau. Smith was uncomfortable as a presidential fire-fighter and believed that prolonged activity might hinder the development of the Budget Bureau as the principal staff arm of the President in fiscal analysis, organization and management, legislation, and budgeting. He was concerned with remaining above the partisan fray, sensitive to but not captive to political pressures. Harold Smith's enduring contribution to the institution of the presidency is illustrated by a December 1945 recommendation by Truman's advisors that the President veto a recession bill which had passed the Congress. Smith quickly informed Truman, "I know that most of your advisors are recommending a veto, Mr. President, perhaps because they know your desire, but I may want to recommend that you sign it." Truman responded, "Well, make your recommendation, so that I can see both sides."[63] Harold Smith's education of President Truman had succeeded. Under his leadership the President's institutional conscience stood ready to serve the interests of the presidency.

The thirteen months following Smith's resignation were ones of uncertainty for the Budget Bureau's future, and the appointment of an anonymous bureaucrat from the Treasury Department did little to forestall the worst fears of the BOB staff. Smith had recommended Assistant Director Paul Appleby as his successor in a "personal and confidential" letter to President Truman. Smith tried forcing Truman into a corner on Appleby's selection. The Director explained that if Appleby were left as Acting Director "there will not only be a question in his mind as to your intentions, but a feeling of uncertainty will quickly spread to the staff." The Budget Director was determined to maintain continuity in leadership.

> "With my leaving reluctantly as I do, an alarming large number of men have come to me and have indicated that they would feel free to leave. During the past few days, I have sensed for the first time the real depth of the esprit de corps that exists in the Bureau of the Budget. It is this staff that serves you as President day in and day out. There are many men of superior qualifications who can easily be attracted elsewhere, but would not work in the government except in the BOB.

> "The staff has great confidence in the leadership of Paul Appleby. He is particularly good in stimulating, and in my judgement he is unequaled in handling a staff agency such as this."[64]

Smith concluded his memorandum by explaining that he could be so frank with the President because "I have your interest at heart." But on July 25, 1946 James Webb was selected by President Truman as the new Director of the Bureau of the Budget. President Truman even forgot his Budget Director's name at the press conference announcing Webb's appointment. The press conference proceeded as follows:

> "Q. Mr. President, are you ready to announce the new Director of the Budget?

> "The President. Yes. I forgot that. [Laughter] That is—I had so many things a while ago that some of my papers got lost. I will tell you who the new Budget Director is going to be, if I can find the papers down in here."[65]

At the time James Webb was serving as the Executive Assistant to the Undersecretary of the Treasury Department, and was recommended for the Budget job by Secretary of the Treasury John Snyder. Webb recalled that "this meant that I was not known to President Truman, and I wasn't part of his White House coterie. I was really an unknown, as people said at the time."[66] Many Washington observers viewed Webb's selection as a successful Treasury Department gambit in subordinating BOB to Treasury's control. It was generally assumed that the Office of War Mobilization and Reconversion (OWMR), not BOB, would emerge as the President's central staff agency. While OWM focused almost exclusively on high priority policy matters, its successor, the Office of War Mobilization and Reconversion, ventured into the BOB's responsibilities for administrative coordination and legislative clearance. Neustadt noted that "most Budget staff accepted without much demur, OWM's wartime overshadowing of their coordinating role; they took with far less grace OWMR's widening post-war interventions on the legislative front."[67] Smith was greatly concerned by OWMR's reaching for Budget Bureau functions. OWMR moved into traditional Budget Bureau turf of manpower policy, surplus property disposal, contract settlement, stock-piling, civilian control of atomic energy, and even legislative clearance responsibilities.

Fortune, however, looked favorably on the BOB in November 1946. OWMR was abruptly abolished and the fledgling Council of Economic Advisors was an untested resource. Where only one year earlier presidential competitors knocked jurisdictional shoulders in the EOP orbit, the Budget Bureau now stood alone. Personal leadership would again provide the catalyst for the Bureau's response. James Webb, it turned out, was an exceptionally imaginative and entrepreneurial bureaucrat whose success rested on his managerial capabilities. Webb saw this policy vacuum and decided that the Budget Bureau's institutional staff could help the President by dealing directly with Truman rather than through intermediaries. In their first meeting, the President "started off by telling me that I had a hard job, but, next to members of the Cabinet and the President, the most important job in the government, that he was counting on me to give him the facts as I saw them, regardless of pressures, that he would make

39

any decisions to deviate from facts but did not expect me to try to anticipate him or color the facts to suit him." Truman told Webb, "I will not make any decisions about you behind your back—you can count on that."[68]

The White House staff was relatively small in size and totally dependent upon what the President passed them rather than being in the mainstream flow of the papers. As BOB Director, Webb was in this flow. The White House soon turned to the Bureau for help in their projects and, most significant, borrowed people from the BOB for ad hoc assignments. Roger Jones observed that "Webb saw immediately the need to make himself and his organization indispensable to the President and he proceeded to do so with great dispatch, great vigor and with tremendous intelligence. He made the Bureau staff available to the White House staff to work with them. He volunteered to take some of the difficult problems the President faced back to the Bureau for further analysis."[69] These problems included drafting legislation on Taft-Hartley, the Employment Act of 1946, the problems of the Fair Employment Practices Commission, Medicare, unification of the Armed Services, the National Defense Act, and harnessing atomic energy for peaceful purposes.

The most important institutional change of the period was in the Budget Bureau's traditional legislative clearance role. Prior to 1948 legislative clearance had been fundamentally negative in character. Neustadt observed that "Webb turned to his machinery for legislative clearance as a prime means of focusing staff efforts to help meet the President's needs."[70] Teams from the BOB and White House worked long hours in formulating, for example, the Housing Act of 1949, the Social Security Act Amendments of 1950, and the President's veto message of Taft-Hartley.

By establishing the Bureau's Office of Legislative Reference as an extension of the White House, Webb proved that an institutional watchdog was needed. When the White House staff was preparing the President's 1947 State of the Union Message, delivered at the opening session of the 80th Congress, Special Counsel Clark Clifford requested ideas on labor-management relations. Webb informed Clifford that he had some individuals in the Budget Bureau (David Stowe, Ross Shearer, and David Bell) who might be of assistance. Clifford requested that the group provide him with a draft of their ideas on possible labor legislation. Clifford also requested that the group keep track of the Taft-Hartley legislation, and they later assisted Clifford in drafting the veto message after the bill had been enacted. Clifford soon wrote to Webb ("My dear Jim") that the efforts of Bureau staff "were of great value. I was particularly impressed with the dispassionate manner in which Mr. Stowe and his colleagues analyzed highly controversial issues, and I feel that their recommendations concerning those issues showed great technical competence and very excellent judgement."[71]

Unlike Harold Smith, Webb brought staff members with him when he went to the White House. Webb even held "dry runs" before going across the street so that the Budget Director and his assistants would be prepared for any problem that Truman wanted answered. Webb recalled that the procedure of bringing his staff to the White House meant that he "did not have to try to master every single detail on every complex subject, nor did these men have to rely on memoranda from me as to what the President wanted done. This made for a very effective working relationship."[72]

Webb developed the policy of helping those people on whom the President relied. By 1950, Stowe, Bell, Neustadt, Enarson, Andrews, Kayle, and Hechler of the BOB had crossed the street to the White House. According to Webb, "the President needed help and they had knowledge. We were not jealous or concerned. We knew that we had a very secure place."[73]

Webb abandoned Smith's concept of the Director's role as the point of intersection between institutional and personal presidential perspectives. He believed that the fundamental difference between himself and Harold Smith was his predecessor's protectiveness of the Bureau, whereas Webb thought that the Bureau was strong enough to stand on its own feet and swim in perilous waters. Webb acknowledged that "Harold Smith was a great recruiter. He was a very sound, theoretical thinker. He understood the doctrine of public administration and he left there people like Lee Martin (Estimates) who was a genius with respect to the figures. He could take a spread sheet as big as that sofa and point his finger to the number that was wrong. Fred Bailey (Legislative Reference) was a wonderful man . . . Don Stone (Administrative Management) was a great recruiter of young people into the Bureau and a terrific advocate of public administration excellence through all of the government. You had a tremendous number of good people. I didn't bring in any senior staff people into the Bureau. I used the ones who were there."[74] In doing so, James Webb bridged the gap between the BOB and White House in the program development area.

Under Webb's directorship the Budget Bureau's role in Congressional relations was vastly expanded. In 1947, through the process of "direct referrals," Republican Congressional Chairmen could inquire what the Democrats intended on various legislation. The opening of channels with the 80th Congress allowed Congressional Committees to request from the Budget Bureau "views on pending bills, at the same time that requests for views were sent to the agencies."[75] President Truman appointed Roger Jones, a registered Republican, to serve as liaison with the 80th Congress. Jones noted that "President Truman wanted an institutional relationship with an opposition Congress. He wanted them to know what his programs were, how he wanted to go about doing it. We were expositors, explanatory people. We were not peddlers of doctrine."[76]

While Harold Smith was responsible for creating the modern Bureau of the Budget, James Webb was instrumental in redirecting Bureau staff work into the program development process. Many observers view the Webb period as the golden age of the Bureau of the Budget. In addition, most observers agree with Webb's observations that President Truman "used the staff work of the Bureau of the Budget in a pioneering way to develop and strengthen 'the Institution of the Presidency.' "[77] For example, an unpublished Brookings Institution report prepared for the 1960 transition observed that "under the strong leadership of James E. Webb and [Webb's successor] Frank Pace, the Bureau reasserted its primacy as the 'general staff' of the President. Relinquishing none of its control over the budget-making process, the Bureau moved into a new era of staff support. Starting cautiously in 1947 and becoming more systematic and comprehensive each year, the Bureau worked out a partnership with the Special Counsel to the President in developing affirmative legislative proposals, covering all aspects of foreign and domestic policy."[78]

Nevertheless, while BOB and White House staff worked in tandem on the President's legislative program, "the theoretical line between the institutional and personal presidencies that separated the Executive Office from the White House also became more blurred as the Budget Bureau provided staff and services for presidential assistants."[79] Moreover, as the "best" of the Budget Bureau's program component took jobs across the street, they could not easily be replaced, and few returned to their institutional roots. Life on the other side often proved too action-oriented. The institutional effects of these exchanges are difficult to assess. Was this a case of utilizing an institutionalized Bureau or stripping it of valuable assets? In this case the Bureau's performance escaped real scrutiny because policy was non-operational and the Budget Bureau's contribution to it via budgeting and legislation raised few of the questions about BOB competence or responsiveness that arose in later periods.

Moreover, throughout the "heyday" of BOB-White House domestic policy interactions, the Bureau's internal organization showed signs of sluggishness when responding to the demands of a constantly changing environment. As the Bureau's workload increased in direct proportion to the government's involvement in domestic and foreign policy, Harold Smith's original blueprint for five divisions providing analyses on all issues entering the Bureau proved inadequate. The Bureau's search for an organization which best served its needs illustrates the BOB's response to an activist presidency while seeking to satisfy its internal organizational requirements.

As its government-wide workload increased, the Budget Bureau's organization along functional lines prevented effective interdivisional coordination. The five divisions provided horizontal perspectives on problems raised by federal agencies, but many problems now cut across several divisions and no Bureau coordinating mechanism existed short of the Director's Office. A person in Legislative Reference usually had to find and then personally coordinate his work with the responsible individual in Administrative Management or Estimates. It was not uncommon for BOB staffers in different divisions to be working on the same problem without knowing what the others were doing. The implications for discharging staff responsibilities were evident to V. O. Key, then a BOB staff consultant, who reported that "the internal organization of the Bureau is such that it is extremely difficult to manage the Bureau in the sense that all its resources can be brought to bear expeditiously on a given problem within a reasonable time. [Consequently], the Director's resources in advising the President are limited by the internal organization of the Bureau."[80] This was especially troublesome because with OWMR abolished the BOB was unprepared for the central coordinating responsibility.

In August 1947 Webb asked Elmer Staats to study the Bureau's internal organization.[81] Staats's report argued that the Bureau's effectiveness "as a staff agency of the President" depended upon its internal coordination and that "no matter how the Executive Office is organized, or what the role of the Bureau becomes in the Executive Office, we need to give serious consideration to significant changes in our organization." Staats noted, "it is significant that the Bureau has not been strong enough to be considered the primary

44

long-range coordinating agency for the Executive Branch."[82] The Bureau's institutional requirements called for a structure which would enable the Director to bring together all resources bearing on a particular problem; deal with problems on both a government-wide and a functional basis; provide the Director with increased staff for reporting effectively to the President; provide a central focal point for internal program coordination, program planning, and facilities for continuous improvement of internal Bureau management; enable the staff assigned on an agency basis sufficient time and facilities to deal with special problems in the functional area concerned.

Staats informed Webb that "there has been an understandable reluctance to open up the subject of major reorganization. The fear expressed is that there is no 'best way' for organizing the Bureau and that any reshuffling might well result in more harm than good, [even though] there has been among the staff of the Bureau a great deal of discussion and not an inconsiderable amount of criticism of our organization."[83] Staats recommended that Webb establish the position of Executive Assistant as the central position of program coordination in the Budget Bureau. External demands from the White House, Congress, and the agencies required that the Bureau have a general manager. The Executive Assistant would provide the Director with a right arm in managing the Budget Bureau and represented an important step toward coordinating internal work flows with external demands. While the Director and his assistants were pulling double harness with the White House, in principle, someone would be managing the BOB.

BOB staff subsequently undertook a self-study in November 1948 designed to provide a well-coordinated program analysis function; treat management and budget as a common process; establish an attack on basic problems of the budget process; strengthen the organization around the Director for total Bureau management; develop and utilize top staff more effectively; and, perhaps most important, provide opportunities for changing habit patterns and installing new points of view.[84]

The group recommended a new type of Assistant Director operating *not* as a Division Chief but as a *leader* in programming and coordination. A proposed Office of Program Review responded to Director Webb's program emphasis within the Bureau and would focus on "the Bureau's responsibility for staff work on the President's program—as a major responsibility, not a subsidiary of the Estimates process" and would be staffed with a small group of highly competent program analysts.

Webb's resignation following the 1948 election and the reform recommendations of the Hoover Commission pushed the BOB self-study recommendations to the background. In June 1951,[85] however, the BOB's Budget and Planning Office initiated another review of the Bureau's organizational requirements. This study group proposed reorganizing the major divisions on a functional (clientele) basis by dividing the Bureau into major operating divisions and staff offices. Coordination would be facilitated and manpower needs reduced by locating all personnel working in a functional area in the same division. Specific problems would no longer need the attention of several specialists. The number of divisions contacting one agency would also be reduced and the staff offices would insure that long-range planning received adequate attention. (The primary disadvantage was the possibility that immediate problems and budget issues might drive out long-range planning and management concerns.)

The Budget Bureau's institutional performance is determined by the degree to which it can provide the Director with thorough staff work in his dealings with the President. This, in turn, is conditioned by the Bureau's internal coordination. The BOB's 1952 reorganization revealed the way a presidential staff agency sought to achieve internal coordination in response to external demands. By 1952 external demands necessitated a fundamental reorganization of the Bureau's staff services and the Bureau reorganized its budgetary, fiscal analysis, and administrative management work along functional lines. A 1959 BOB self-study report acknowledged that the 1952 reorganization "resulted from many years of thought and discussion concerning the most effective ways of meeting the Bureau's responsibilities as the principal institutional staff arm in the Executive Office."[86] Five new operating divisions (replacing Estimates) were established to work directly with the agencies on program, budgetary, economic, and management issues. The five former divisions were reorganized into four offices, each headed by an Assistant Director. The offices assumed responsibility for Bureau work on important government-wide problems; advised and assisted the Director in the establishment of Bureau policies and programs; and coordinated and provided guidance to the Divisions in their functional responsibilities. (Appendix Two, C.)

The reorganization was based on the key assumption that all other Bureau functions were related but subordinate to production of the budget. This premise seriously weakened the Budget Bureau's ability to support the President in areas other than budgetary. By abolishing the Fiscal Division and emasculating the Division of Administrative management, the reorganization destroyed or seriously impaired those BOB units with across-the-board outlook and organized them around the budget divisions, which were agency oriented. Problems immediately manifested themselves in the management area and before long the Budget Bureau became open game for presidential reform groups, the first of which was President Eisenhower's Committee on Government Organization, chaired by Nelson Rockefeller. Moreover, by the end of Eisenhower's first term, the "golden days" had become the "dark days"; and the Bureau's very purpose was being questioned.

THREE

Rigidification of a Staff Agency, 1953-1960

Few political observers could be certain what would happen to the Budget Bureau when President Eisenhower assumed office in January 1953. As the first Republican President to be elected in twenty-one years, Eisenhower confronted a Budget Bureau that since its transfer to the EOP in 1939 had served only Democratic Presidents. Many of the Bureau's top career staff had been recruited twenty years earlier by Harold Smith. Could these civil servants respond to Eisenhower's interests? Would there be a wholesale purge of partisans? BOB official Elmer Staats recalled that, "this was a crucial period in the history of the BOB. Under a different set of circumstances, a different Director could have gone far toward dismantling the staff of the BOB and altering its role as the principal staff arm of the President."[1]

President Truman and his Budget Director Fred Lawton were determined to prevent any dismantling of the Budget Bureau. Lawton, the first BOB careerist appointed as Budget Director, believed that Truman's selection of him at a time when the President was close to the decision of not seeking re-election meant a continuation of the Bureau as it had evolved over the years, regardless of who won.

Immediately following Eisenhower's 1952 election victory, President Truman requested that General Eisenhower send a representative to the Budget Bureau so that the President-elect could be fully informed on the Fiscal Year 1954 Budget —a budget Eisenhower inherited in January, 1953. The Fiscal Year 1954 Budget ran from July 1, 1953-June 30, 1954. The incoming administration inherited the Fiscal Year 1954 budget, the supplemental budget for Fiscal Year 1953, accumulated and unfulfilled fiscal obligations from prior years.

Eight days later Joseph M. Dodge, a Detroit banker, arrived in the Budget Bureau as Eisenhower's Budget Director designate. Dodge's arrival initiated a sequence of remarkable examples of maintaining continuity in the institutionalized presidency during a time when partisan change might have led to the Budget Bureau's demise.

Dodge's first priority was to learn everything he could about Truman's 1954 budget. He was given complete access to information and was free to discuss budgetary matters with BOB staff members. Dodge sat in on BOB staff meetings so that he would know why certain decisions were made, although he had no decision-making responsibility. Eisenhower had explicitly instructed Dodge not to give the appearance of responsibility for budget decisions because Dodge's very presence at these sessions might restrict Eisenhower's future budget choices.[2]

With these ground rules established, Dodge spent the next two months studying the Fiscal Year 1954 budget and experienced firsthand the institutional contribution made by the career staff of the Budget Bureau. Despite general suspicion by the incoming Republicans of a predominantly Democratic federal bureaucracy, Dodge informed Eisenhower that the Budget staff was objective, nonpartisan, and highly qualified to serve the interests of the new administration. Elmer Staats noted that Dodge was "tremendously impressed, for example, by the fact that we had no record of the politics of any of our principal staff of the Bureau of the Budget. . . . I think he was impressed by the amount of information and the objectivity of the staff work of the Bureau. He was, therefore, able to say to President Eisenhower when he assumed office that he did not wish to see any basic change in either the staffing or the direction of the work of the staff of the Bureau of the Budget."[3] Moreover, the "best proof of that pudding," Roger Jones of Legislative Reference recalled, "came in the eating, when, within less than sixty days, the Budget [Bureau] took the new set of instructions from President Eisenhower and Mr. Dodge, revised that Budget, cut it back, depending on how you count it, somewhere between 10-12 billion dollars, and sent it forward to the Congress, with subsequent enactment by the Congress with very little change."[4]

Between November 1952 and February 1953, Dodge called most of the incoming Cabinet members into the Budget Bureau for briefings on their departmental programs and budgets. These forums enabled the Bureau to prove its worth as a supplier of institutional knowledge while at the same time socializing the new administration on its programmatic responsibilities. For example, the incoming Secretary of Commerce, Sinclair Weeks, was on record against the St. Lawrence Seaway project. Roger Jones explained to Weeks that both major parties were committed to the project, and that the committees of Congress looked to the Commerce Secretary for leadership in legislation. Weeks reversed his opposition and one of the earliest legislative accomplishments of the Eisenhower administration was the St. Lawrence Seaway. Significantly, it was the BOB, not Weeks, which took the lead on the St. Lawrence Seaway legislation. Senior BOB staffers drafted the bill *and* were the principal administration witnesses and negotiators with Congress.

The Bureau's "education" of incoming Cabinet members continued with Secretary McKay of Interior. McKay was opposed, in principle, to federal construction of electric power capacity in multipurpose public works projects. Jones recalled that "we had to review in detail the rationale (and necessity in some cases) of including power features in some pending reclamation projects to which both Republicans and Democrats were committed."[5]

Fresh in office, Eisenhower failed to utilize the Bureau in a program-planning capacity for the 1953 legislative year. But he soon discovered that he needed a program if his leadership was not to be usurped by McCarthy, Taft and others not of the modern Republican persuasion, and that the Budget Bureau could be of major importance in attaining that goal. In May 1953 the Budget Bureau sent out its annual call for estimates from the federal agencies for Fiscal Year 1955 with specific requests for programmatic departures. Neustadt explained that renewal of section 86 in 1953 represented "not an Eisenhower innovation but a bureaucratic continuum, an attempted restoration of routines, an action taken on the Budget's own initiative without advance assurance as to either agency response or ultimate White House reaction."[6] The results were staggering. By September 1953, some 300 agency and department proposals arrived in the Budget Bureau. Many of these recommendations included pet programs that had floundered in the Truman administration. Others represented proposals for supplemental funding of ongoing programs—many of which the new administration was on record as being against.

The White House, overwhelmed by this bureaucratic initiative and its results, turned to the Budget Bureau for help. A series of meetings were initiated between BOB staff and their White House counterparts to determine which proposals could be adopted into the President's State of the Union Message. Roger Jones assumed responsibility for briefing the White House staff on the history and merits of most proposals. These briefings were offered in "institutional terms," leaving policy judgments to partisans. Jones recalled that "there came about almost a fierce dedication [on the part of the White House staff] to keeping me in the role of telling both sides of the story."[7]

White House aides first checked Jones's version of the story. Convinced that he was both loyal and accurate, they went to the President for guidance. Several of the more partisan policy recommendations—social security, taxation, agricultural assistance, and foreign aid—were scheduled for Cabinet discussion. Preparation for these Cabinet meetings was elaborate. Cabinet members were briefed on their program area and dry runs were held. Presentations were given over several Cabinet meetings, with the President often leading the discussion, and culminated in the formal presentation of Eisenhower's 1954 legislative program—his program, not McCarthy's. As Neustadt remarked, "The Presidential program,

51

once, perhaps, a questionable undertaking of a necessary chore, was now becoming a prime political imperative, its relative readiness a godsend, one expects, to the regime."[8]

The Budget Bureau's institutional contribution to the immediate needs of a new President, and the provision of continuity to the presidency, represented a fine beginning for a once suspect staff agency. The BOB 1963 *Staff Orientation Manual* noted that "the Bureau carried on its role as institutional staff under the new administration as it had previously worked under the old."[9] The Bureau's initial success, however, was not converted to influence in policy-making. Far from a legislative activist, Eisenhower viewed the Budget Bureau as his agent for obtaining control of spending trends. This emphasis was evident in his selection of bankers and accountants as Budget Directors. Eisenhower's first two Directors, Joseph Dodge (January 22, 1953 to April 15, 1954) and Rowland Hughes (April 16, 1954 to April 1, 1956), were bankers, and Percival Brundage (April 2, 1956 to March 17, 1958) and Maurice Stans (March 18, 1958 to January 20, 1961) were accountants.

Eisenhower evidently considered the Budget Director an important administration official, since Dodge was the first Budget Director to hold formal Cabinet status. Eisenhower wanted Dodge to be his eyes and ears from within rather than from without. Cabinet status for the Budget Director may not be in the Director's best interest. "The inevitable result," argues Roger Jones, "was, you pulled the Budget Director down so that he was just one among ten other guys. The Budget Director could no longer stand above what the Cabinet was doing because he was right there when it was going on."[10] James Webb recalled that, "I never went to Cabinet meetings. I tried to avoid getting invitations. I was an intermediary between the President and a Cabinet officer. I didn't want them ganging up in the Cabinet room and saying, "Now Mr. President, if it weren't for this Budget Director we could get a lot of things done.' "[11]

Dodge supported his career staff, enjoyed an excellent working relationship with the President, but differed significantly from the Smith-Webb view of BOB staffing. For example, in 1953 testimony before the House Appropriation Committee on the Bureau's own appropriation, Dodge argued that, "the Budget Director, while proposing reductions in requests on the part of other agencies [could not] come before you and insist that his agency must have more money." The printed version of the Budget Bureau's budget for Fiscal Year 1954 was $3,700,000, but Dodge proposed cutting it to $3,450,000. Representative Cotton, sounding like an apostle of Harold Smith, informed Dodge that his committee was well aware of the BOB's special mission and the Budget Director should not fear asking for more money. "I would rather see you have a larger budget and have a staff sufficient to do the job you think necessary, than simply, for fear of certain criticism, artificially reduce the budget and thus impair your efficiency."[12] In meeting the standards for this "self-imposed parsimony," Dodge reduced many Budget Bureau operations. The first to be eliminated were the BOB's four field offices in Chicago, Dallas, Denver, and San Francisco. This amounted to a cut of nineteen employees and $202,000.

Dodge was succeeded by Rowland Hughes, a budget technician with little interest in the Bureau's broader staff role. Hughes was unwilling to trust his career staff, and, as one former official noted, "we Division Chiefs had a difficult time keeping the troops lined up, willing to come to work. It was a bleak, awful time." Hughes eventually resigned because of pressures relating to his role in the Dixon-Yates controversy, and was succeeded by his Deputy Director, Percival Brundage. Brundage, a former accountant and executive for Price-Waterhouse, was a staunch defender of his agency but served as Budget Director while Eisenhower was recovering from a major illness. Lacking the forcefulness and leverage to get to the President through either Sherman Adams or Treasury Secretary George Humphrey, Brundage focused on the Bureau's role in improving governmental accounting practices and investigating different ways for measuring the budget (the National Incomes Account Budget, the Administrative Budget and the Cash Budget).

By the final months of Hughes's tenure as Director, however, it was evident to senior career officials that their agency was not effectively discharging its responsibilities. Bureau staff had little idea what the Director was thinking, there was little communication from the Director's Office to senior career officials, and staffing arrangements themselves were inadequate. Subsequently, in February 1956, an internal evaluation of the Bureau's organization was initiated under the supervision of Assistant Director Percy Rappaport. Rappaport requested that all Division and Office heads provide their views on Bureau organization and staffing problems. Senior officials were extremely candid in their comments, as indicated by one official's request that his comments "be treated with appropriate confidence. They have not been seen by any members of my staff."[13]

William McCandless of Budget Review wrote to Rappaport that, "there are some basic problems affecting the whole Bureau which need attention." McCandless observed that many of the problems originated in Hughes' office. The Bureau "need[ed] a new sense of direction . . . a redefinition of its objectives in the broadest terms. It need[ed] to know what the Director thinks is important for the Bureau to do, to what aspects of the total Bureau job the Director attach[ed] the greatest significance, and his concept of relative agency and Bureau responsibilities in the areas where the Bureau functions. . . . The internal cohesiveness of the Bureau need[ed] to be improved by better communications with, use of, and support of Bureau staff through systematic organization channels."[14]

William Carey, of the Labor and Welfare Division, reflecting uneasiness with the lack of communication between career division chiefs and the Director's Office, had "long mourned the exclusion of the division chiefs from the Director's staff meetings, and not merely for reasons of pride. . . . I doubt that there have been half a dozen occasions in the past three years where division chiefs have known what transpired at a morning staff meeting. I can't believe that this is as it should be. . . . As matters stand now, we deal with the Director on spot problems. We do not have opportunities to tune in on his wave length where the general direction of the Bureau's business is concerned. . . . There is no substitute for the responsible desk officers of the Bureau to participate in the daily conferences on the bridge."[15]

R. M. Macy of the International Division wrote to Rappaport that the Director rarely acknowledged good staff work and it was "no secret that the morale of a number of budget examiners around the Bureau is rather low because they feel that much excellent staff analysis received little or no attention from the Director's Office in reaching budget decisions."[16]

By April 16, 1956 Percy Rappaport notified the new Budget Director, Percival Brundage, that several changes were required to improve BOB organization and procedures.[17] The BOB needed to redefine its objectives, clarify lines of authority, and increase opportunities for staff self-expression. Primary among the recommendations was the clarification of the Director's responsibilities, improved communication of the Director's point of view to the staff, and better utilization of senior career officials in staff assignments.

While Brundage made every effort to implement these goals, his most significant decision was selecting Maurice Stans as Deputy Director, because on March 18, 1958 Stans replaced Brundage as Budget Director. The change in leadership, as described by one senior official, was "like opening up all the curtains in the building and letting the sun shine in. There was confidence, there was leadership, everything turned around. . . . I used to think that if Kennedy found a strong Budget Bureau when he arrived it was because of what Stans did to put it back on its feet after four awful years."

With Sherman Adams now departed from government, the Budget Director had direct access to the President. In addition, Eisenhower was very upset by the $12-billion-dollar deficit in 1958 and he wanted it brought to an end. Eisenhower and Stans agreed that the government should balance its budget, but to do so would require strong presidential backing of the Budget Director. Eisenhower wrote in his memoirs, "advisors had warned me against moving, in a single year, from a recession budget in the red by an estimated $12.9 billion to a one in balance. . . . Under Maurice Stans, the Budget Bureau went to work. With a determination and dedication that amazed as much as it delighted me, he deluged the Cabinet and—when possible—the public with statistics that made truly fearsome ogres of the gaudy promises of the spenders."[18] Stans recalled that in preparing the Fiscal Year 1960 budget "the President backed me up all the way through in Cabinet meetings and everywhere else. He wanted the agencies to accept my judgment as much as possible because he wanted to hold the budget down. They said we couldn't do it but we balanced the budget."[19]

Most former Budget Bureau officials with whom I talked invariably noted, "If Dodge had remained," or "when Stans arrived." Dodge and Stans placed their faith in the BOB career staff and worked directly with the President. Dodge, a banker, and Stans, an accountant, viewed their roles as master mechanics or financial comptrollers. Between 1953-1960 a Budget Director's task was to balance the numbers. They were technicians responsible for advising the President how government could be run for less money. Unlike their predecessors in the Roosevelt and Truman administrations, they were not public administrators, and, unlike their immediate successors in the Kennedy and Johnson administrations, they were not policy-oriented economists.

Being responsive to Eisenhower's desire to balance the budget, however, did not mean that the Budget Bureau as an institution staff agency was living through another golden decade. This very responsiveness to Eisenhower's goals prevented the Bureau from developing a forward-looking attitude. In August 1960, for example, as part of the BOB's

56

preparation for the next Presidential transition, Bureau official William Carey requested that Division Chiefs provide him with a list of all possible basic criticisms which might be lodged against the Budget Bureau's "stewardship" from 1953-1960. The most interesting response came from Phillip Hughes of Legislative Reference, who described the effects of Eisenhower's policy goals on the Bureau's institutional image as "completely negative in its outlook and incapable of constructive deliberation, and with a dollar sign as its only criteria. . . . It seems to me that the strenuous efforts of the past few years to balance the budget have probably cast the Bureau, as an institution, and its personnel in an essentially negative role."[20] Hughes recommended that "ways should perhaps be sought of emphasizing the fact that the Bureau does not instinctively respond 'No' but rather seeks the right answer within the framework of Presidential policy." (e.g., responsiveness to presidential needs is our raison d'être)

Many observers have equated the Bureau's responsiveness with a decline in influence. A 1960 Brookings Institution transition report observed that following the Bureau's "auspicious beginning" during the 1952 transition, the Bureau's influence "slowly waned. More and more, the Budget Bureau has tended to become the executor of decisions made at the White House, in the Cabinet, and in the National Security Council."[21] Those who believe that the BOB should play a more active role in program formulation obviously view the Ike years with anethema. As Hess observed, "the Budget Bureau continued to do what it had always done, but it was not just as central to the making of policy."[22]

When Eisenhower left office in 1961, he took credit for three balanced and two proposed balanced budgets, believing that he had achieved a major victory against the "big-spenders." This negativism placed the Budget Bureau in a role of the President's "nay-sayer." To argue that the Bureau's influence in making policy declined under a President who did not want many policies may miss the point. By 1960 the

Budget Bureau staff had lost certain intangible qualities: bold initiative, creativity, flexibility, the feeling that being quick on one's feet mattered to the White House. Ironically, the authors of a working paper prepared for a 1967 BOB self-study asked, "Why did parts of the Bureau adjust more easily to the negativism of the Eisenhower than to the activism of Kennedy or Johnson? . . . We find it incredible that a number of the Bureau's top career staff now look back at the Stans/Eisenhower years as a golden era to which we should return."[23] This illustrated the fundamental paradox of the Budget Bureau as a presidential staff agency (and provides the central analytic focus for the post-1961 assessment of the Bureau's response to the needs of activist Presidents).

The Bureau's problems, however, began well before 1961. Between 1956-1960 the Bureau was under full-fledged attack by President Eisenhower's Advisory Committee on Government Organization (PACGO) chaired by Nelson Rockefeller. PACGO believed that the management processes in the Executive Office needed improvement, and that to do so the BOB needed to be substantially reorganized or abolished. The case study offers a fascinating example of the Bureau's fight to keep its self-perceived status as "first among equals" in the EOP.

PACGO believed that the President's staff facilities for administrative management were ineffectively organized. Under the term "administrative management" PACGO grouped the full range of Budget Bureau functions: budget preparation and administration, legislative clearance and coordination, organizational improvement, management improvement and efficiency research, accounting improvement, and coordination of statistical programs.

The growth of the federal government's responsibilities had "increased the volume and complexity of the President's management functions," but "an adequate, balanced organization to help the President with these expanding tasks" had not evolved concomitantly.[24] Program coordination was a major managerial problem. Because institutional arrange-

58

ments that fell within the purview of a single executive department or agency did not exist, temporary staff arrangements were established in the White House to deal with these matters. The ad hoc and temporary nature of these groups meant that the President or his closest aides had to personally integrate and coordinate the program recommendations with budgetary policy.

In January 1957, PACGO made its first recommendation to the President for improving Executive Office management responsibilities. The President's management problems could be alleviated by establishing an Office of Administration in the EOP. The Director of Administration would be given broad responsibility for assisting the President in "general administrative matters in the Executive Branch."[25] The proposed Office of Administration would be located in the chain of command between the President and the (now reorganized) BOB, with the Director of Administration reporting directly to the President and assisted by three deputies and several staff assistants from the BOB.

Budget Director Percival Brundage vehemently opposed this proposal. Brundage argued that the Director of Administration would create an added layer between the Budget Director and the President.[26] President Eisenhower agreed with his Budget Director. In a meeting with PACGO, the President said their idea "had great appeal" but "the action would tend to downgrade the top men of the Budget, of the planning office, etc., who can be obtained now largely only because they have the right to come in to the President."[27] Eisenhower instructed PACGO to develop an alternative for improving management processes in the EOP.

On October 10, 1957, Rockefeller responded to Eisenhower's request and wrote to the President that PACGO still in principle favored the reorganization of Executive Office management activities into an Office of Administration "so that you can rely on one man for the coordination of all such activities."[28] But because this necessitated statutory changes, including amending the Budget and Accounting Act, and might involve controversy and delay with "no certainty as to the final outcome," PACGO had a "second best" proposal. This was the appointment in the White House Office of an Assistant (or Deputy Assistant) to the President for Management with coordinating and not operating responsibilities. The Deputy Assistant would aid the President in coordinating the work of the BOB and other units in the EOP. The Deputy Assistant would report to the Assistant to the President (who at the time was Sherman Adams).

Budget Director Brundage was no more sympathetic to PACGO's compromise proposal than to the original recommendation. The Budget Director viewed the plan as a downgrading of the Bureau's Office of Management and Organization. Brundage registered his official dissent in a memorandum to Sherman Adams, enclosing a copy of Executive Order 8248, which, according to Brundage, "clearly places the responsibility for administrative management squarely in the Bureau of the Budget."[29] Brundage wrote to Adams in a strong defense of the Office of Management and Organization that:

> "The provisions of Executive Order 8248 make it clear that the concept of the Executive Office which has governed its organization and procedures for nearly twenty years has been one in which (1) the Budget Bureau has been the President's staff and coordinating agency in the "Management" field and (2) the White House Office and Budget Bureau have been parallel units of the Executive Office performing different duties for the President. *Specifically, staff of the White House Office are not 'interposed' between the President and the Budget Bureau.*"

PACGO staff director Arthur Kimball believed that "the Budget Director's memorandum proceeds on the basis of several obvious misconceptions as to the Committee's intent."[30] Jerry Kieffer and John Kennedy, staff members of PACGO, believed that Brundage's analogy of the Bureau's status in the EOP was an "inconsistency so often practiced by the Budget staff. . . . The Budget Bureau is supposed to be a principal staff arm of the President, [but] really is not a part of his staff but exists separately and apart from him (thus safe from political retribution and restaffing after a change in Administration)."[31]

The Budget Bureau's response to PACGO's proposals is a textbook illustration of Miles's Law—"where you stand depends upon where you sit."[32] From the chair of the BOB Director, PACGO's recommendations were viewed as a downgrading of the BOB's Office of Management and Organization and another potential barrier between the Budget Director and President. From where PACGO was seated, the recommendations were seen as restructuring the existing management processes to reduce the President's workload.

On March 17, 1958, Director Brundage retired and was succeeded by his deputy, Maurice Stans. By April 31, 1958, the Executive Management Act, 1958, had been drafted in the White House. The bill established an Executive Assistant to the President for Administration who would coordinate, supervise, or perform "functions now assigned to the Director of the White House-Executive Office administrative management organization."[33] The Office of Executive Assistant for Administration would be responsible for developing and coordinating the federal budget; the President's legislative program; staff work in budget, personnel, organization, and management; and planning and program evaluation.

Assistant Director Finan believed that these recommendations "reflected a lack of understanding of the way the Budget Bureau carries out its functions." Finan favored "re-integrating the organizational talent of the Budget Bureau and placing it under a strengthened organization and management unit."[34] PACGO had grown accustomed to Finan's objections, and on April 22, 1958, Kimball advised the committee that the "Budget Bureau staff is still strongly opposed to the idea."[35]

In a meeting with Sherman Adams, Stans agreed that the BOB's management responsibilities needed to be improved and Stans recommended that an Office of Executive Management (OEM) be established by reorganizing the BOB.[36] Director Stans favored any changes that would enlarge and strengthen the BOB without altering the relationship of its Director to the President. The Budget Director's position was based on four propositions: (1) The Bureau of the Budget could and should be upgraded; (2) he would oppose the interposition of anyone between the head of the reorganized Bureau and the President; (3) he did not have any strong feelings of what the name of the organization should be, but thought that the word "management" should be in its title; (4) he was in favor of putting within the upgraded organization the personnel function and other management and organization functions loosely attached to the White House, together with some responsibilities in helping the President with program planning.[37]

PACGO agreed that Stans would be the first Director of OEM. The OEM was to have a Director, a Deputy Director, and not more than six statutory Assistant Directors. The statutory functions of the BOB would be transferred to the Director of OEM. The new agency would have five divisions responsible for budget preparation and administration, legislative clearance and coordination, personnel management, organization and management, and program planning.

Plans for implementing the OEM were initiated in the White House. In spite of Director Stans's support of the plan, Assistant Director Finan was persistent in his opposition to any reorganization of the Bureau's management functions. Finan believed that "a more detailed Presidential explanation as to why [Eisenhower] was abolishing the BOB"[38] was needed. In another textbook example of Miles's Law, PACGO staff member Jerry Kieffer wrote to Milton Eisenhower that Finan misunderstood PACGO's intent:

> "[Finan's view] stems from the original Budget staff reaction that this whole reorganization is designed to downgrade the BOB. Actually, while the present institution called the BOB would be abolished, the entire range of activities now in the BOB would be enhanced by the greater concentration of

functions under the Director of Executive Management. . . .
We see no reason for [Eisenhower] to offer a detailed justifi-
cation with regard to the fate of the BOB."[39]

On November 28, 1958, Kimball wrote to the committee
members that the Budget Bureau staff was trying to sabotage
the reorganization plan. Observing that "the Budget Boys
never give up," and "here we go again," Kimball explained
that Finan, who was responsible for drafting the technical
aspects of the plan, had "reverted to the earlier Budget staff
approach, which the Committee (with Mr. Stans' concur-
rence) did not favor."[40] Finan had simply renamed the BOB
the Office of Executive Management and transferred to it the
Office of Personnel Management and other EOP units. Contrary to the Stans-PACGO agreement, moreover, Finan's
draft authorized the OEM Director and not the President to
appoint the statutory Assistant Directors of OEM.

Meanwhile, Robert Gray, Secretary of the Cabinet, notified all members that on the following day, December 12,
1958, President Eisenhower with the assistance of Dr. Flemming would brief the Cabinet on "what is intended in the
Presidentially-approved reorganization of the Bureau of the
Budget."[41] Gray's memorandum explained that an Executive
Order would create OEM except for its Budget Bureau elements. The Budget Director would be named as Director of
OEM and, simultaneously, a Reorganization Plan would be
sent to Congress transferring the BOB to the OEM. Gray
requested that the memorandum be handled on an "eyes
only" basis and returned to him immediately after the Cabinet meeting.

At the Cabinet meeting the draft of the reorganization
plan was judged to be inadequate and Director Stans was
asked to personally draft the reorganization plan. Stans's
draft emphasized that BOB was being renamed because "the
name BOB obscures the full range of duties of that agency
and is an impediment to the achievement of its management
role."[42] Kieffer believed that the reorganization should be
much more than a renaming of the BOB. A Cabinet meeting

63

was called for the next day to discuss the Budget Director's draft. Kieffer wrote to Gray that, in setting the meeting's agenda, several subjects needed "greater emphasis," because Stans's draft "clearly indicates a Budget Bureau attempt to portray reorganization simply as a renaming of the present BOB."[43]

By January 28, 1959, only eight days after Director Stans had submitted his draft, staff director Kimball wrote to Dr. Milton Eisenhower that the BOB was on the verge of defeating PACGO's recommendations because PACGO had been "outmaneuvered by the Budget staff."[44] Kimball did not know, however, that Stans was preparing an internal self-study of the Bureau to serve as an "institutional" response to PACGO's recommendations.

On January 30, 1959, Director Stans informed Budget Bureau staff that an internal self-study of the functions, operations, and workload of the Bureau would be initiated on February 2, 1959.[45] The self-study group could scarcely have been a stronger bastion of veteran BOB staffers. The group consisted of eleven individuals with an aggregate of 246 years of experience in the Bureau (an average of 22 years each). Director Stans requested that the group submit their report by May 1, 1959. This necessitated an intensive work schedule, often from 7:00 a.m. to midnight. The conclusions of the study group offer a fascinating example of how two groups (PACGO and the study group) looked at the same problem and because of different perspectives and interests recommended entirely different alternatives.

The 149-page report and its sixty recommendations illustrate the Bureau's perception of its future as a reinvigorated BOB. The study group was primarily concerned "with the Bureau of tomorrow—in the advancing years of the Twentieth Century," and identified what it believed were the fundamental long-range institutional needs of the Budget Bureau:

"The Bureau must have "*flexibility*" in its operations—to assist the President in anticipating and meeting complex problems in a rapidly changing world. . . . The premium will be on *looking ahead* and *being prepared before* crises arise.

"The Bureau will be able to serve adequately only to the degree that it becomes versatile in fast-moving situations. *Now is the time to emphasize the development of that versatility.*

"The Bureau must be an institution concerned with 'growth' . . . *An organization must grow* or stagnate. Growth does not require the attainment of a large size, for the Bureau will always necessarily be a relatively small staff agency. Emphasis should be upon '*maturity*'—the high quality and professionalism of the staff. The Bureau, however, must continue to evaluate its capacity to do its traditional job. That evaluation must assure that the Bureau continues to be *dynamic* and *grows* in harmony with the growth of its tasks."[46]

The study group believed that, once these long-range needs were met, the BOB would transform itself into a "new style" Bureau. The Bureau needed to "reorient its way of life to keep pace with the new challenges." A new style Bureau could "become a *positive* influence in helping the President guide the direction of the changes of tomorrow."[47] The key concept to emerge from the 1959 study was "staff anticipation," characterized by the seizing of opportunity and forward planning.

"The doctrine of staff anticipation is that the staff has the obligation of never permitting the chief to be caught unprepared or to be surprised. It is their obligation to anticipate possible future developments and to initiate the necessary planning and study so that the chief has well in advance the considered expert opinion of the staff and their recommendations on the advantages of the possible alternative lines of action, together with their recommendations of what they consider to be the best alternative solution. . . . It is the substance sparking all Bureau effort and providing a more adequate response to challenge."[48]

Staff anticipation, or the ability to foresee emerging problems, represented the study group's belief that the Bureau needed to transcend its 1953-1960 "green eyeshade" role. In

65

the covering letter of its report, the study group informed Stans that they had "taken a long-range look at the Bureau as an institutional staff arm of the President,"[49] and concluded that if the Bureau developed a forward-looking style of staff anticipation it could again provide the President with anticipatory staff services. Director Stans "agreed fully with the thesis that 'staff anticipation' must be safeguarded," and "that this quality of the Bureau as an institution goes far to explain the value of its work to the President."[50]

It is interesting that these senior BOB officials, most of whom had served under Harold Smith and/or James Webb, returned to a general staff concept of the Budget Bureau's role. After all, the Eisenhower (banker/accountant) years did much to destroy the Bureau's creativity, flexibility, and forward-looking attitude. The Bureau survived the 1950's by becoming an enclave, and recommendations for a "new style" Bureau could not restore these lost qualities. Rather, the BOB institutional dilemma called for the influx of new blood and career rotation patterns.

Nevertheless, the next President and Budget Director believed that the BOB of 1961 could again become the BOB of 1947. David Bell, President Kennedy's first Budget Director and a former Bureau staffer during the "golden days" under James Webb, believed that the Bureau had not been used to its fullest capabilities during the Eisenhower years. For example, at their first meeting, Bell informed Kennedy that "it seemed to me that during the Eisenhower years the Budget Bureau had degenerated into something little more than an accounting staff, and that was not my impression of what a President needed or should have from the Budget Bureau."[51] Moreover, the Budget Bureau presented itself as a logical appendage for program-planning rejuvenation under an activist Democratic President in the mold of Roosevelt and Truman. In this case, however, policy would become operational and the Budget Bureau would be held responsible for its implementation and coordination.

66

Responding to Activist Presidential Leadership: The Bureau of the Budget That Could Never Be, 1961-1969

During the 1960 transition, President-elect Kennedy's advisors recommended re-activating the Budget Bureau as the primary program planning unit in the EOP. Richard Neustadt (another former BOB staffer under James Webb) recommended that Kennedy's broad legislative goals required a Budget Director "soaked in substance . . . a broad gauged policy advisor, not an accountant. . . . The reason why your man ought to be program-minded, not a cost accountant, is that national or presidential needs may call on him to urge you to say 'yes.' . . . Your man should have sensitivity to the requirements and limits of staffwork in an 'institutional' staff role." Neustadt added that the Budget Bureau was "still the nearest thing to institutional eyes-and-ears and memory, encompassing all parts of the Executive Branch, which you will have available to you when you take office."[1] A Brookings Institution transition report offered similar advice in recommending that Kennedy's Budget Director possess "sensitivity to political and administrative as well as financial and organizational matters." The Brookings report informed the President-elect that "at times in the past, the Bureau has been the preeminent organizer and watchdog of the presidential program. Presumably it could become so again—it would be forced into the role, in fact, if there were a significant effort to reduce the proliferation of White House staff that has accrued over the past 8 years, and if the President should rely on the Director for general matters of program administration."[2]

The 1960 transition provided the Budget Bureau's first test as a presidential resource and the BOB staff again educated the new presidential staff on the workings of government. Phillip Hughes of Legislative Reference recalled that "early after the election, a number of us within the Bureau sat down with key members of President Kennedy's staff to familiarize them with the institutional processes."[3] President-elect Kennedy assigned program development responsibilities to his long-time aide, Theodore Sorenson. Waiting for Sorenson was a "Kennedyopedia," a list of each policy statement made by Kennedy during the presidential campaign, and its relation to proposed or ongoing programs (a Nixonopedia was discarded after the election). Working teams consisting of Sorenson, Myer Feldman and Lee White from the White House, Bell, Elmer Staats (a "walking encyclopedia" for program proposals), and Phillip Hughes from the Budget Bureau worked in tandem, establishing the President's initial options for his legislative program, culminating with the President's 1961 State of the Union Message.

The President-elect wanted to move quickly with his New Frontier legislation. Under Sorenson's direction, twenty-nine transition task forces were established on topics ranging from national security, organization of defense, natural resources, wheat, cotton, agricultural surplus abroad, space programs, education, health and social security. By Inauguration Day, twenty-four of the twenty-nine task forces had reported back with their proposals. By February 2, legislation calling for an extension of unemployment insurance, an increase in minimum wage, aid to dependent children of the unemployed, and aid to areas of chronic economic stress were forwarded to the Congress. These were followed by health and hospital care legislation, including health insurance for the aged through social security, a federal grain bill, grants to the states for school construction and teacher's salaries, highway programs, Peace Corps, housing, and a general farm bill.

The Bureau's staff work in anticipating the needs of a new President again demonstrated the institutional value of a career staff. The BOB 1963 *Staff Orientation Manual* acknowledged that "the institutional character of the Bureau was again reinforced by the smooth transition to the Kennedy administration."[4] Director Bell emerged from the transition period as a trusted Kennedy assistant, and the White House staff started looking to the Budget Bureau's Office of Legislative Reference as a resource in the program development process (much like relationships during the Webb Directorship).

In principle, Kennedy viewed the Budget Bureau as an integral institutional component in his advisory structure, but he viewed the Budget Director as an even more valuable special assistant. The program orientation of Budget Directors David Bell and Kermit Gordon (the first in a series of economist Budget Directors) enabled them to serve as personal advisors to Kennedy and as adjuncts to Theodore Sorenson's Special Counsel office. The White House gradually centralized program development responsibilities in Sorenson's office and the Budget Director became a leading participant in the program development process. Unlike the Smith and Webb period, however, less attention was paid to the everyday management of BOB, partly because most Bureau resources were geared to service a legislatively active President and, as Sorenson noted, Kennedy "was always more interested in policy than administration."[5] Moreover, the President's Budget Directors possessed little sustained interest in organization or management problems. A working paper prepared for the BOB's 1967 self-study stated that "Bureau Directors since [1960] have been program rather than management oriented. They have reflected the predominent inclination of their bosses. Moreover, the White House style during this period had tended to emphasize the individual rather than the institution. The quality and individual competence of Bureau Directors during this period has been so great that the Bureau's overall stature in the minds of the President and the Congress has probably never been higher. Paradoxically, the institution has suffered internally during this same period because of the lack of attention paid to its day-to-day management."[6]

While these patterns emerged in the Kennedy administration, its toll upon the Budget Bureau did not fully materialize until 1966, when the strains of the Great Society were evident. To the casual observer it might have appeared that the BOB, as an institutional resource, was being utilized to its fullest possible extent. Moreover, the Budget Bureau's institutional contribution in the post-Kennedy assassination period fueled such perceptions of BOB indispensability.

When President Kennedy was assassinated on November 22, 1963, the budget was at a critical stage. Agency requests had been submitted and the budget review process was already underway. Budget Director Kermit Gordon immediately sent a memorandum[7] to President Johnson describing the status of the 1965 budget and included a review of BOB general staff services. Gordon emphasized that the Bureau of the Budget was "a staff agency to the President which, by tradition and in fact, has no constituency other than the Presidency and no obligations which complicate its allegiance to the President." The Budget Bureau stood ready to "meet your needs" in the areas of (1) public expenditures, (2) pending or proposed legislation, and (3) government organization and management. "On any of these matters," Gordon explained, "we can provide you, in short order, with a statement of the relevant facts, a statement of the pros and cons of particular courses of action, and our recommendations." Gordon added that he was to have met with President Kennedy the following Wednesday to review Gordon's recommendations on agency appeals. The Budget Director noted that "despite the fact that the time is late, I know that you will want to make this budget your budget. Accordingly, I hope that I can sit down with you very soon to present the major policy issues involved in the budget and obtain your guidance on how we should proceed in formulating a budget which embodies your views." Gordon enclosed a budget timetable allowing December 2-20 for final decisions on agency programs under existing legislation, December 26 for decisions on proposed legislation, January 9 for locking up the Budget message, and January 19 for submitting the Budget to Congress.

On the same day William Carey, Executive Assistant Director of the BOB, wrote to Presidential Assistant Bill Moyers, providing "a handy checklist in case the Bureau can help out as questions arise."[8] The memo identified several integral BOB responsibilities for helping the President manage the Executive branch, including the issuing of executive orders and proclamations, reviewing commitments made by President Kennedy, preparing speeches, messages and legislative drafts, checking facts and budget data, advising and drafting government organization plans, coordinating and clearing legislation, mediating agency disputes, Congressional liaison work, and information retrieval on current government programs.

On November 25, Gordon sent a detailed memorandum to the President reviewing the background and status of the 1965 Budget.[9] President Kennedy had agreed with Wilbur Mills to hold the deficit below 9.2 billion; preliminary estimates for 1965 indicated that to do so required expenditures to be below $101.7 billion. Agency submissions for 1965 were $109 billion, a new obligational authority $119.6 billion, personnel requests were being screened separately.

The President soon met with Treasury Secretary Dillon, Chairman of the Council of Economic Advisors Walter Heller, and Budget Director Gordon and insisted that expenditures be reduced below $100 billion as a show of good faith to Senator Byrd and other Congressional conservatives who, in return, would support the proposed tax cut program. BOB staffer John Young recorded that "the issue of $100.5 billion without a tax reduction or $100 billion or less with $11 billion tax cut was clearly put before the group by the President."[10]

Johnson's economic advisors questioned the necessity of a $100 billion or less budget. CEA Chairman Walter Heller believed that the Administration could "readily defend a fiscal 1965 budget in the range between $101 and $102 billion,"[11] but Johnson recognized that Harry Byrd would not be sold on Heller's new economics. The President told his economic advisors that in spirit he wanted an expanding economy but also needed the $11 billion tax cut and unless the budget was reduced to $100 billion, "you won't pee one drop."

Budget Director Gordon went to work at trimming the Budget. (Johnson once described the Cabinet as 9 salesmen and 1 credit manager.) The Budget Director informed Johnson that "the prospects for bringing the budget down to the neighborhood of $100 billion look a bit better than they did last night."[12] McNamara was trying to reduce Defense expenditures by $600 million, and $300-400 million might be cut through various accounting procedures and Gordon's sight-draft technique. Gordon warned the President, however, that further reductions might prove harmful in the long run. "Let me reiterate, however, that the 101.5 figure with which we have been working already embodies a large number of tight program decisions which will provide outcries from the wounded agencies and their clientele."[13] For example, to get $101 billion, Gordon cut all new irrigation starts and made drastic cuts in reclamation and REA.

Nevertheless, Johnson remained steadfast in his insistence that the budget be reduced. President Johnson personally reviewed each agency budget request and between December 2, 1963 and December 12, 1963 met with Gordon twelve times. Gordon recalled that "I think the effect was to convince the country that here was a man in control and determined to follow a policy of economy and parsimony. I'm sure he felt that it did him some good. It worked with the Congress. Byrd was never a strong supporter of a tax cut in face of federal deficit but he muted his opposition in light of the very impressive efforts the President was making to hold down the budget."[14]

President Johnson's personal impact on the 1965 budget

was staggering. After final figure juggling, total expenditures were reduced from 101.5 billion to 97.9 billion. The 1965 budget included a decrease of 1,200 in Federal employment; a reduction of more than $500 million in expenditures (only the second administrative budget in 9 years to show such a reduction from the previous year); and a reduction of more than $4 billion in obligational authority. These measures cut the deficit from $10 billion to 4.9 billion.

On January 20, 1964 President Johnson signed the 1965 budget, telling BOB staff that in his 32 years of government service "I don't think I have ever seen more diligence or dedication in any single endeavor than the work that went into the budget that goes to Congress tomorrow. I spent many hours, many days, with the men that you folks here sent over as messengers, who did the real work, and it is a tribute to you and it is a tribute to our country that we can have people like you."[15] Johnson always remembered Gordon's efforts, as evidenced by the President's 1965 letter accepting Gordon's resignation. The President observed that "from the first hour I occupied the Presidency, you were at my side with sound counsel and a never-failing common-sense. . . . You gave me unmeasurable help in restricting our spending below the $100 billion mark. . . . You have helped comfort me and give me strength. I will miss you greatly."[16]

On February 26, 1964 President Johnson signed the tax bill, vindicating the strategy of the $100 billion or less budget. Moreover, between November 22, 1963 and January 20, 1964, the Budget Director and his staff provided President Johnson with invaluable assistance in his budgetary responsibilities. The Budget Director, having passed the test by fire, gained entrance into LBJ's inner advisory circle.

The Bureau's responses to the immediate needs of President Johnson present a classic case of institutional staff work in the EOP. Unlike the Bureau's regular transition role which benefits from months of preparation, the post-assassination period is unmatched for thorough staff response. Yet, succeeding in what it did best, relying on its institutional mem-

73

ory, knowledge, and objectivity, the Bureau may have planted the seeds for its institutional exploitation. President Johnson recognized a good thing and soon learned that not only could he trust his Budget Director, but that the Bureau was a good place for staffing task forces and giving ad hoc management problems because assignments were never turned down or ignored. The Budget Bureau soon became a dumping ground for all sorts of Presidential problems that should have gone elsewhere. The BOB, however, had few options because its very existence depended on its responsiveness to Presidential demands (compared to needs). This was the beginning of the end for the Bureau of the Budget as an institutional staff arm and by 1968 it was hard to distinguish personal from institutional staff responsibilities in the Executive Office. The proliferation of New Frontier-Great Society domestic legislation placed an inordinate strain on the administrative machinery of the central government, and especially on the Bureau of the Budget. By 1967 the Bureau's future was under evaluation by a BOB study group and the Heineman task force on the Organization and Management of Great Society Programs. Both groups identified serious institutional inadequacies in the Budget Bureau's performance during the 1960s, a period during which the White House valued individual rather than institutional talents.

It all began innocently enough. In 1965 Joseph Califano replaced William Moyers as the White House coordinator for the President's legislative program, establishing *both* interagency as well as outside task forces. Under Califano's guidance, task forcing assumed a regular format: in the early spring, Califano requested that department and agency officials forward new ideas *only* for the upcoming legislative year. Califano and his staff then visited several universities, talked to scholars about new policy departures and problems facing the nation. In July, these ideas were incorporated into a program development book containing all new proposals, unfulfilled presidential commitments and pending legislation.[17] The contents of the book were screened by a group

74

usually consisting of Califano, Doug Cater, Harry McPherson, Larry Levinson, and James Gaither from the White House; Schultze and Phillip Hughes from the Budget Bureau; and the CEA chairman. By the middle of August task forces were established, with a BOB staffer serving as the administration liaison.

President Johnson assured task force members that their work would be held in strict confidence and therefore they should not be concerned with either political or budgetary restrictions in making proposals. Task force reports were sent to the BOB's Office of Legislative Reference (OLR), which served as a principal liaison with the White House staff. Within two days the BOB divisions affected by task force proposals furnished the Director with a memorandum summarizing the task force recommendations, the probable impact of each recommendation on the next budget, how each recommendation related to the affected agency's budget, and action recommendations. The Director either returned the report to the division or office for more details, or sent five copies of the Budget Bureau recommendations to the White House, where the Califano group made its final recommendations to the President.

Task forcing produced several important policy departures, but created their own administrative havoc. Two days or two weeks was not enough time for the Budget Bureau to provide careful program analysis. In 1965 and 1966, for example, no formalized arrangement existed between the White House and Budget Bureau for costing of task force proposals, leaving many good ideas without money. James Gaither of the White House Domestic Affairs staff observed that the White House staff "had not paid much attention to the budget in the development of the legislative program for 1967. And while we had everything priced out and showed all the dollar figures on the outline and in the presentation to the President, we never had really checked to make sure that all those dollars were really in the budget. . . . So we had a wild six or eight hour meeting with Califano and Schultze and we had to try and put some money into the budget for the key elements of the President's program in 1967."[18] It was not unusual for the Budget Director, already locked in with his decisions on HEW, to have Califano call and say something like "we've got a presidentially approved recommendation from a task force for $6 million additional funds, come on over." William Carey reports that "after a couple of years of task forcing, the practice of uniformly posting Budget Bureau staff as executive secretaries lapsed because there were too many task forces. They almost began to outnumber the staff of the Budget Bureau."[19]

Task forcing revealed a failure to link legislative and budgetary issues into a continuous process. By 1967 task force proposals and their budget add-ons involved large uncontrollable resources. New ideas were developed without any respect for fiscal resource constraints and there was substantial overlap between task force proposals and those already in the regular budget process. Among the most frequent criticisms were that task force recommendations varied with those submitted to the Budget Bureau through regular channels; agencies could not accommodate proposals in their budgets; the costing of task force proposals was not done uniformally; and there was no provision for exploring future costs of programs while in the proposal stage.[20] A 1967 BOB self-study staff assessed the administration's task force effort as "fitful and ad hoc," compressed into a hectic two- or three-month period, with little time or incentive for the serious consideration of objectives, much less the costs and benefits of alternative approaches. The paper concluded that "the natural tendency of a political process to treat the politics of a problem rather than the problem itself meets no counterpoise, with the result not merely that the national or Presidential interest may be unrepresented, but that the special interest to be served may be served poorly."[21] The philosophy of the time was: pass that law, get that appropriation, and worry about it later. William Carey observed that "the task force routine, with all its other merits, was regarded and treated principally as a kind of instant policy blender to whip up tasty concoctions to meet the message schedule in January. There was no way on earth to integrate task force activities with budget assumptions and planning figures, and for sheer disarray the double exercise of task forcing and budgeting had no peer."[22]

What began as a mechanism for tapping new sources of talent and ideas had developed by 1967, into "feverish policy formulation outside the context of fiscal reality." Carey, a key participant in the process, reported that "when the budget came under such strain that money could not be provided for programs already on the books, to say nothing of new ones emanating from task forces, nothing was done to turn off the task forces. Each year they grew in number, churning out new and tempting proposals, while on a separate circuit the budget was being cut under the President's personal and attentive direction. When the time came in mid-November to sort out and price the outputs of from 40 to 50 task forces, with no money in sight, the confusion was unexampled."[23]

The premise that bureaucratic channels were too slow for capitalizing on Johnson's 1964-1966 legislative majority supplied the rationalization for centralizing policy-making initiatives in Califano's Domestic Affairs staff. The Budget Bureau, formally the initiator of such responsibilities, came under White House control as its agent. While White House staffers viewed certain "individual" BOB officials as remarkably competent, *the Bureau* as an institution was viewed as unresponsive to a White House staff with 10 programs for every idea.

BOB officials were subsequently "called to Joe's office," where the emphasis was action-oriented. Kermit Gordon recalled that "a good deal of time was spent in Califano's office sitting around the table with agency and Cabinet members thrashing out decisions on program matters."[24] Budget Director Zwick observed that "at times I thought that [the Domestic Affairs Staff] was trying to get too close to the Budget Bureau's responsibilities and trying to increase program budgets . . . they tried, by working with the examiners, to influence the decision making below me, above me and alongside me."[25] When Charles Schultze resigned in January, 1968, it was rumored that he was upset at being pre-empted by Califano's operation. A "confidential" memorandum from Califano Assistant Larry Levinson to Press Secretary George Christian lends support to these allegations: "At Joe Califano's request, I talked to Joe Kraft. Kraft, I believe, is going to write a critical piece about Charlie Schultze's resignation and he may cite one of the reasons the fact that the Joe Califano staff has pre-empted much of the Budget Bureau's programming and planning function."[26]

Matthew Nimetz of the Domestic Affairs Staff explained that "the BOB as an institution tended to be suspicious of any new program . . . the people of the Budget Bureau—I think the younger people find the older examiners are very restrictive. They are brought up in the old view of the Budget Bureau: it's not creative, it's just analytical of the agencies, and this adding more and more programs just sort of strikes them as wrong."[27] Nimetz cited BOB examiners in Indian Affairs taking "a very narrow attitude of the government's role toward Indians. A presidential task force recommended that Indian School Boards be established in every Indian school; these were Federal schools to be run by Indian parents. The President, the Commission on Indian Affairs, Califano, and Secretary of the Interior, Stewart Udall decided to give the Indians control because they could not do any worse than the federal government in running the programs. The Budget Bureau examiners, however, kept changing the wording in the bill to "advisory" school boards because they believed that the Indians should not be allowed to run them. Nimetz later learned that BOB examiners were telling the Bureau of Indian Affairs to hold off on these school boards until they saw how the first few worked. "They were really trying, in my view, to kill the whole program, and doing it through the budget process of just saying, 'You're spending money; we've got to see how it works,' this and that. . . .

Here the Budget Bureau, which usually helps us, is working against us. It was very difficult to get anything done."[28]

The President's 1965 cost reduction program provides a good example of White House staff suspicion of the BOB. The program was aimed at reducing government costs, financing new programs, and offsetting increases. This was the type of assignment LBJ liked to give the BOB. Some White House assistants believed, however, that the BOB could not provide the type of staff work necessary for protecting the President. On May 27, 1965, White House Assistant Dan Witt wrote to Jim Jones concerning his "reactions, responses and impressions" of the BOB role in the cost reduction program. Witt argued that "for the President's own protection," Johnson have one of his own assistants monitor the program, over and above the Budget Bureau. "Somehow, something must give the President more than the BOB is or will give him."[29]

The suggestion that Johnson protect himself from the BOB's inability to do so was a serious charge for an institutional staff whose existence was predicated on protecting the President. Witt informed Jones that during a recent meeting with the Bureau's management staff

"We were put on the defensive during the first 10-15 minutes. . . . They spent considerable time lecturing us about what the BOB does—although it was unnecessary. . . .

"Seidman has been through many administrations (Truman, Eisenhower, etc.) and appears to be fairly set in his ways. Expressed deeply rooted thinking denoting a lack of flexibility.

"[Seidman, Osborne and Parker] will say things are being done, and actually are, on paper, but are *really* not. No generalist outlook. Little imagination—no creativity. Not stimulated enough, not aggressive enough, not dynamic about it.

"BOB is not manning sufficiently for an effective cost reduction program. I asked what type of organizational structure

79

do you envisage to carry out the program. The answer was 'there we are, Mr. Osborne, Mr. Parker and myself (Seidman). We don't need any special organization.' "

Witt concluded that the BOB was not really excited about the cost reduction production, lacked proper vision, and needed to be "rattled and led." It is difficult to assess the effects of such perceptions on the institutional work product. However, from the manner in which organizational and management problems manifested themselves, we must ask whether "rattling and leading" the Budget Bureau was in the best interests of the presidency. William Carey reports that President Johnson "spent the better part of a year badgering the Bureau Director to assign five of the best men you have to drag advance information out of the agencies about impending decisions and actions so that he could pre-empt them and issue personal directives to carry them out, but the Budget Bureau never came anywhere near satisfying him because its own radar system was not tuned finely enough."[30] Subsequently, White House staff members appeared at agency meetings and frequently took field trips. Perhaps the problem rested in Johnson's refusal to distinguish institutional from personal staff responsibilities. Harold Seidman observed that some members of the Johnson White House still insist " 'Oh, we used the Budget Bureau, we used them extensively.' Joe Califano will say that. *They didn't use the Budget Bureau as an institution. They used individual Budget Bureau staff as legmen to do pick and shovel work.* This was not using the Budget Bureau."[31]

The social programs of the 1960s were radically different and far more administratively complex than previous federal programs. Creative federalism was management at its most difficult and required several federal agencies to cooperate among themselves and jointly with state and local governments on a single project. The Bureau, as a central staff agency with no operating programs of its own, was viewed by operating agencies as a natural vehicle for arbitration and

80

counseling on interagency problems. In response to these administrative problems, the Budget Bureau shifted its institutional emphasis to intergovernmental and interagency coordination. The administrative problems needing solutions, however, were inordinately complex and fragmented. For example, in the area of grant-in-aids alone, considerable overlapping and duplication existed within functional areas: HUD, USDA, and EDA provided grants and loans for water and sewer work; HEW, Labor, HUD, Agriculture, Commerce, and OEO all made education and training grants; VA, HUD, and HEW were all concerned with nursing homes; HUD and Interior focused on open spaces. This high degree of overlap generated its own coordination problems. In addition, there was no rational pattern for matching grant requirements and no consistent national policy on equalization.

By 1966, the poverty program was under criticism for mismanagement and inadequate appropriations. HUD, previously considered the "textbook department" (because all authority is legally concentrated in the Secretary), was becoming an ineffective bureaucracy. Sewer and water programs were being slowed down because of overlapping, competition, and confusion of standards and requirements; activities in aid to education were so scattered and information so difficult to obtain that it was impossible to chart progress; water management responsibility was divided among fifty or more different agencies, independent of central policy guidance; and regional economic development was in chaos.[32]

As jurisdictional and implementation problems emerged in the intergovernmental area, the President, the White House staff, departments, and agencies naturally looked to the Bureau for assistance. The Bureau's official administrative history noted that "the need for new coordinating machinery was there, but the bars to telling someone to 'go out' and coordinate were numerous. From various sources, the Bureau was being asked to do something about these problems."[33]

In December 1965 Budget Director Schultze established a

task force on Intergovernmental Program Coordination chaired by Stephen K. Bailey, Dean of the Maxwell School at Syracuse University. The Bailey task force reported that the management of Great Society programs was "marred by too many instances of confusion and contradiction" and that "the welfare of individual citizens has too often been lost in a maze of interagency and intergovernmental procedures, overlaps, delays and jurisdictional disputes."[34] The task force was emphatic in its recommendation that the Budget Bureau immediately undertake a thorough study of its organization and consider reestablishing field offices. The report noted that "nearly fourteen years have passed since the Bureau last underwent a major introspection and reorganization. *It now needs to develop a clear definition of its role and of its organization and staff requirements under the pressure of new federal programs and responsibilities.*"[35]

The Bailey task force also recommended that the Bureau either increase its staffing in the management area or establish a new office for intergovernmental coordination which would minimize jurisdictional overlaps, systematize grant-in-aid formulae, rationalize agency jurisdiction and policies in open space presentation and outdoor recreation development, make consistent the formulae for reduction allowances, broaden the category of federal grants, and decentralize project decisions of the Office of Economic Opportunity. The recommendation for field offices (which were abolished under Eisenhower) is especially relevant. As new programs proliferated, departments and agencies increasingly came into contact with each other in the field. This inevitably led to problems in coordination, consistency, duplication, and competition.

Between 1964 and 1968 the Budget Bureau requested, and was denied, appropriations for re-establishing its field offices to assist in the coordination of interagency conflict. In 1966, for example, the Bureau requested from Congress an increase to establish an Intergovernmental and Field Project Unit with a staff of twenty-one. The unit would monitor federal-state-

82

local programs at the point of actual operations in the field. In 1967 Budget Director Schultze requested funds for federal field operations, arguing that "the existing staff resources of the Bureau of the Budget are adequate for identifying the kinds of problems that are emerging, they are *not* sufficient to enable the Bureau either to have enough extended field coverage for firsthand observation and analysis, nor to provide the necessary additional time efforts to develop effective solutions. Unless we staff up to work across the board on intergovernmental, interagency, and field problems, there will be increasing dissatisfaction and criticism both in and out of Congress."[36]

Several Congressmen feared that a BOB with field offices would become a high-level ombudsman, federal czar, umpire, or decision-maker in the field, and not a catalyst for working out agreement. Schultze argued that "no Budget Director worth his salt, and I think all of them have been worth their salt, wants to get the Budget Bureau into the position of being an advocate for particular programs or particular solutions, because once you do that, you know, the Bureau is lost in its usefulness to the President. . . ."[37] Despite the Budget Director's guarantee that the Bureau sought to help the President and not operating responsibility, Congress denied all BOB appropriation requests. The same Congress in 1968 indicted the Budget Bureau for failing to do anything about coordination problems in intergovernmental management.

Between June-September, 1966 the Bureau's Office of Management and Organization (OMO) undertook a fact-finding evaluation based on five reconnaissance surveys of problems facing federal, state, and local officials in carrying out intergovernmental programs. BOB staffers visited Seattle, Nashville, Philadelphia, Columbia (S.C.), and Denver, where they interviewed governors, mayors, local officials, and university personnel. The major focus was on "problems they have encountered or are aware of in connection with the administration of Federally-funded programs requiring intergovernmental or interagency cooperation in their application."[38] The results of the survey were disquieting. Bureau staff discovered that administrative problems extended to all levels of government. Most problems were caused by the proliferation of narrow, complex categorial grants and loan programs with a great deal of overlap and interrelatedness.

Perhaps the most complex problem confronting the Budget Bureau was simplifying the application process through which states applied for federal funds. The BOB tried monitoring grant-in-aid programs for consolidation, and simplified the application procedure for multiple grants by making it easier for states and localities to combine federal grants for multi-purpose projects. For example, several federal agencies administered programs associated with the war on poverty. A major problem in the anti-poverty program was that different local agencies would separately approach different federal agencies with grant proposals in related areas such as work programs, training programs, and adult literacy programs. These local agencies did *not* actually exchange basic information with each other and this resulted in waste and inefficiency. The Bureau established a procedure between OEO, HEW, HUD, and Labor whereby local anti-poverty agencies were required to exchange program information and objectives *before* requesting federal funds. The Budget Bureau also monitored the fifteen federal Executive Boards. The BOB Director reported periodically to the Executive Officers Group, and monitored the fourteen City Neighborhood Center programs to test interagency and intergovernmental coordination at the urban level.

By January 1968, however, a Senate subcommittee began studying the organization and management problems of the Executive Branch of Government. Chairman Abraham Ribicoff observed that the "net result of our massive Federal effort in recent years seems to be an instrument of national policy that is unplanned, uncoordinated, unmanaged, and— if these trends continue—unworkable."[39] Ribicoff blamed the Bureau of the Budget for most of the Great Society's administrative failures and recommended that the President "seek authority to establish an Office of Management and Coordination in the Executive Office." Ribicoff labelled the Bureau the "great Sacred Cow of the Federal establishment" and charged that "much of the problem and the blame of what happens in the executive branch falls on the shoulders of the Bureau of the Budget."

Ribicoff was not alone in his assessment of the BOB's response to the management of the Great Society programs. In 1966 the Heineman task force on government organization believed that the BOB was ill-suited as a management staff, and recommended that an Office of Program Coordination be established as a new unit within the EOP. The work of the Heineman task force offers a fascinating assessment of the BOB's response, or lack of it, to the administrative and program demands of the Johnson years.

In 1966 a study of the organization and management of Great Society programs was undertaken by a Johnson administration task force. William Carey reported that Johnson buried the report "in the presidential desk drawer and applied a total embargo on both the distribution of copies and any mention of the fact that there existed such a task force."[40] During the 1968 presidential transition, Johnson's transition coordinator, Charles Murphy, received a request from President-elect Nixon's representative, Frank Lincoln, for a copy of the Heineman report. Murphy wrote to Johnson that because "Joe Califano's feeling is that you should not make the report available to the President-elect but should keep it for your own use," should Murphy give the Heineman report to Nixon? Johnson's answer, scrawled across the top of Murphy's memo, was "Hell, No."[41]

Johnson was keenly aware that the Heineman report had identified shortcomings in presidential staff facilities for inter-governmental management and program formulation, and made several recommendations for strengthening the BOB. The task force rejected the political criticism of those who opposed the goals of the Great Society, but agreed that "or-

85

ganizational criticism was merited" because "insofar as its aim is responsive and efficient government, the Federal government is badly organized."[42] The hundreds of legislative programs developed from 1963 to 1966 had "put a great strain upon absolescent machinery and administrative practices at all levels of government."[43] The President was being judged on his administrative as well as legislative performance because "legislative success . . . [had] added to the administrative burdens of the presidency" by significantly altering the nature of the President's management job.[44]

The Heineman group viewed the President's management job as the "largest and toughest in the world" because, unlike other executives, the President could not give management his complete attention. The task force recognized that "a permanent dilemma for Presidents is that the Presidency has too many dimensions for one man to handle alone yet also is constitutionally indivisible." This fact raised a managerial challenge to the President, e.g., "to keep a firm hand on the domestic tiller by reserving big decisions to himself and by delegating the next level of his work to intimate staff lieutenants who command his full confidence and share his hopes and plans."[45]

Administrative failure did not result simply from the nature of the Great Society programs. Nowhere in the EOP did the President have an institutionalized staff for comprehensive program planning, and consequently, "a portion of our present problem of organization and coordination has been caused by the way new social programs were developed and enacted."[46] The Heineman group identified five major drawbacks in the existing practice of planning new programs. The current practice relied heavily on chance; it focused almost entirely on shaping specialized programs, neglecting the vital job of creating a coherent overall federal program strategy; it tended to neglect emergency or complex problems for which no agency had particular responsibility; it was only loosely related to careful study of social problems and review of existing programs; it provided no regular mechanism for deciding between expansion or modification of existing programs and creation of new ones.[47]

It is important in understanding the Heineman recommendations that the task force viewed management and program leadership as two parts of the same organizational problem. The President needed improved mechanisms for managing intergovernmental programs *and* improved program planning resources for formulating those same programs.

The task force recommended that an Office of Program Coordination (OPC) be established as a new, independent staff unit in the EOP, with a field force organized in ten federal regions. Program coordination was identified as "the greatest unmet need" of the President's management responsibilities. The President needed permanent coordinating instruments in Washington because "the job of program coordination was much too large to be done by a few talented people on a part-time basis," which had been standard operating procedure. The time had come "to institutionalize these responsibilities and provide staff to discharge them comprehensively and effectively."[48]

The OPC Director and staff would assume responsibility for several important management functions in the intergovernmental area by anticipating, surfacing, and settling jurisdictional and program arguments between federal departments; monitoring the administration of Great Society programs requiring cooperation between federal departments; providing the staff focal point in the White House, short of the President himself, for continuing consultation with governors and mayors on domestic programs and problems of intergovernmental cooperation; carrying primary staff responsibility in the Executive Office for longer-term efforts to improve intergovernmental organization relationships through grant consolidation, and harmonization of financial matching arrangements.[49]

The task force considered several alternatives to the OPC, among them a Super Department of Domestic Affairs incorporating all major social programs, and an OPC within the

BOB. Chairman Heineman, Robert McNamara and Budget Director Schultze favored the latter proposal within a "completely reorganized Budget Bureau," but the majority of the task force favored an independent EOP unit. The Bureau was judged as ill-suited for discharging the President's most critical management functions, and should completely relinquish responsibility for intergovernmental coordination.

The Heineman group had well-articulated reasons for locating the OPC outside the Budget Bureau. Domestic program coordination, they argued, is "a large job with short-term operational as well as long-term intergovernmental systems development dimensions. We doubt that it would get the necessary emphasis if incorporated with BOB's two main functions—program evaluation (budget) and program development."[50] The OPC's success depended upon its ability to influence line agencies in the implementation of federal programs. It was a day-to-day and immediate problem of program coordination, far too demanding and politically sensitive to break into the BOB's already highly rigorous, formalized budgetary and legislative clearance cycle with its requirement that legally mandated deadlines be met.

The President needed not only a management control instrument, but also an institutionalized staff for problem definition, program design, and program development. Four years of task forcing, ad-hoc problem solving, and under-funded social programs had undermined the quality of legislative performance. The Heineman group viewed the program development problem as equal to the President's managerial headache. "Just as the President must coordinate programs that are going on today, he needs to look ahead—to ask broad and penetrating questions beyond the concern or purview of line agencies, to spot neglected or emerging problems and to plan and develop social programs which resolve these questions and meet these problems."[51]

The task force recommended that an Office of Program Development (OPD) be established within a reoriented Budget Bureau and headed by a Presidential appointee of

Executive rank. The OPD would assist the White House staff in the program development process by analyzing complex or emerging problems; keeping close touch with the nation's best research efforts; designing, reviewing, and proposing modifications in government programs aimed at domestic problems; stimulating better analysis and program development in the executive departments; stimulating the establishment of, and frequently staffing, presidential commissions and task forces; relating individual programs to a general administration strategy and evolving priorities.[52]

The OPD was to be located within the BOB, on the assumption that "a substantial reorganization of the Bureau of the Budget be undertaken with a view of widening its responsibilities and revising its priorities."[53] The Heineman report emphasized that "reorganization should speed up sharply the Bureau's transition from intelligent reaction to departmental demands to active, independent leadership in program development that supports and is responsive to the President and his perspective."[54]

Chairman Heineman favored renaming the Bureau of the Budget the Bureau of Program Development and Management. A staff paper prepared by Allen Schick recommended that program planning become the central responsibility of the Budget Bureau. Schick argued that the Bureau would have to "reexamine its mission and purposes and its role as Presidential staff," and that the Bureau "must become the center for policy studies in the EOP."[55]

It is significant that these 1966 reformers sought to institutionalize program development and not program coordination in the Budget Bureau (Nixon's Ash Council would recommend the exact reverse). By locating the OPD within the Budget Bureau, especially if the legislative clearance functions of the Bureau's Office of Legislative Reference were consolidated with long range problem analysis and program planning, the annual budget and development of the President's legislative program would be performed under the same roof. The task force believed that their recommendations would not solve the President's management problem. Instead, they were intended to be tools with which the President could enforce overall coordination of federal programs. The report acknowledged that these recommendations "should be seen not as final answers but as steps to strengthen presidential managerial authority and leadership where it now is most needed."[56]

The final report of the President's Task Force on Government Organization was submitted to the President on June 15, 1967. President Johnson refused to take any action on the recommendations and ordered his staff to keep the document secret (Heineman believed that reorganization was to be the first priority of Johnson's second term, and at the time there was no hope of Congressional approval).

Johnson's refusal to act on the Heineman recommendations presented the Budget Bureau with an opportunity to fend off further outside reorganization efforts. In early February 1967 Phillip Hughes, Deputy Director of the BOB, recommended that the Bureau undertake an internal self-study because the BOB needed "a critical analysis of its responsiveness and effectiveness in serving the President and the executive departments and agencies."[57] The most recent BOB reorganization had occurred in 1952 and the last self-study in 1959. Hughes acknowledged that "external demands and the nature of the problems facing the organization have changed considerably since those times."

The Deputy Director identified several reasons for undertaking an evaluation. Outsiders were questioning the Bureau's effectiveness; the BOB was not anticipating or meeting several important challenges facing the President; some Bureau units had "lost their sense of direction"; the President's reliance on task forces suggested that the Bureau was perceived as inadequate for meeting heavy demands on the President; career-development patterns and imbalance in turnover produced a personnel structure characterized by a degree of superannuation and the loss of effective people.[58]

A steering group, chaired by Director Schultze, and composed of individuals from outside as well as inside the BOB was established to oversee the survey. Schultze acknowledged that "only through such a review can we be sure that we are discharging our responsibilities to the President and to the departments and agencies effectively and efficiently."[59]

The steering group staff was given responsibility for developing working papers on problem areas in the Bureau. The steering group members met seven times between March and June 1967 to discuss these working papers, recommend revisions, and prepare their final proposals. A staff summary, developed through a process on consensus building, was submitted in lieu of several individual reports. The numerous and often broadly frank staff working papers, however, provide a valuable "insider" perspective on Bureau-White House relations during the 1960s.

On March 26, 1967 the steering group met for the first time to discuss the BOB's role and mission. It was no coincidence that the initial topic for discussion was the concept of the BOB's role as a general staff agency for the President. While the traditional role of the Bureau involved preparing the budget, over the years an important role in providing general staff work for the President had developed. The working paper listed five evolving general staff functions performed by the BOB for the President and the White House. These included defending administration positions; providing managerial intelligence for the President as to what is going on in the Executive Branch; providing presidential directives and actions in regard to individual departments and agencies; providing across-the-board actions to improve the management of the Executive Branch; and providing early warning information on potential problems of significance to the White House or the President.[60]

The steering group debated whether the Bureau was "living up" to these general staff responsibilities. Several members argued that while the formulation was accurate, the real problem was that, since 1961, the intensity and complexity on *demands* for general staff work had increased. Several fac-

91

tors were identified as contributing to the exploitation of the Budget Bureau as a presidential staff agency.

1. An inability of the White House staff to keep pace with the changing role of the presidency and size of governmental programs, including their intergovernmental aspects.
2. Increased requirements at the Presidential level to obtain a resultant view of government problems that cut across several of the traditional departments and agencies.
3. More important public policy questions that cut across agencies, thus requiring Presidential involvement.
4. A general increase in tempo at which governmental processes appear to work.
5. Marked overlapping of programs and program responsibility in the domestic area.
6. The Bureau [is] the *only* place where one can find a continuous flow of reporting, of government-wide information over a significant span of time.
7. There is a need for the President and the White House staff of a point where "loyalty is not divided."[61]

Moreover, because this general staff role was an evolving one, the Director had no institutionalized support to which he could turn. By failing explicitly to acknowledge a general staff concept in Bureau structure and processes, the Director was personally involved as a presidential fire-fighter. The steering group compared the 1963-1967 period with the 1939-1942 (Smith) period in the Bureau's existence (depression-war crises). "In this period, the Bureau had to face up to handling the situation either by 'beefing up its capabilities' or 'going outside.' The decision at that time was to increase markedly the Bureau's capabilities by bringing in a considerable number of outsiders ('new blood')."[62]

A staff paper argued that while the BOB's traditional role was "help[ing] the President manage the Executive Branch, in ways that his department and agency heads, and his personal staff, usually cannot," this "traditional role" incorporated a "traditional style" characterized by "a body of doctrine, myth, and habit—a way of life . . . a negative, critical approach rather than a positive, creative one; preoccupation with formal, *action-forcing processes in Washington* rather than the solution of problems in the field; the doctrine that the Bureau serves an abstraction called 'the Presidency' rather than an individual President."[63] It was the Bureau's traditional *style* (not its key traditional *role*) that gave truth to charges that the Bureau was "green eyeshade" or "dog in the manger." Moreover, the 1967 steering group reached a conclusion similar to the 1959 concept of staff anticipation and called for abandoning this traditional style, not its traditional role.

The study group identified fifteen presidential staff functions then performed by the Bureau. These included problem definition; policy formulation; program design; program evaluation; efficiency evaluation; development of tactics; communicating and defending the President's positions; exercising government-wide coordinating authority; establishing and maintaining coordination machinery; ad hoc problem solving; liaison activities; reporting on Government activities; general information, intelligence, and early warning; technical assistance and information to agencies, and government-wide promotion of PPBS.[64]

It was evident that the Bureau was not adequately meeting all these demands. The solution was to identify real presidential priorities and to refuse all assignments that did not directly support the Bureau's responsibility as a personal, permanent staff to the Director and President. The study group recognized that the Bureau could not "be in the business of providing services to the entire Federal Government. The record shows that the Bureau often fails when it tries to be the fountainhead of wisdom on a highly technical subject. Even where it is possible, it can no longer afford the resources required. Implementing this concept will require conscious decision not to do things even though the Bureau could make a contribution."[65]

Other aspects of the Bureau's general staff work did not

mesh with the BOB's traditional role. The Bureau's role in operational coordination, for example, illustrated an evolving general staff function that did not support the BOB's traditional role. By operational coordination the study group meant "ad hoc problem solving, the exercise of immediate coordinating authority, and political communication and liaison."[66] Principal activities included coordinating related federal domestic programs and intergovernmental programs; exercising leadership over operating machinery to coordinate intergovernmental programs (neighborhood centers, model cities); expediting action on domestic programs; maintaining a liaison with the Federal Executive Board (FEB), field offices, Governors, Mayors and other officials; defending and communicating the President's position to federal and state officials; and identifying potential coordination problems.

Operational coordination, because of its proximity to state and local politics, was heavily political and threatened the BOB's traditional role. After all, how long could "a career staff of civil servants help the President handle his state and local constituency without losing its reputation for being impartial and nonpartisan? The question is not academic. At some point, the very viability of the institution will be jeopardized."[67] Many Bureau staffers, however, resisted this operational coordination role because it involved the Budget Bureau in intensive contact with political processes and was regarded "as not being in keeping with the traditions and professionalism of the Bureau."[68] While Bureau staffers needed to possess political sensitivity and awareness, political activity threatened the BOB's traditional value. The same applied to the Bureau's information-warning-defense functions. Distinctions were needed between managerial intelligence versus political intelligence because, "a Bureau of the Budget that becomes heavily involved in supplying political intelligence to one President may not be trusted by his successor to provide intelligence on any subject."[69]

The study group staff also conducted extensive interviews

with a cross-section of BOB personnel. Listed below are a sampling of BOB staff comments.

1. *The Bureau lacks a clear sense of direction and purpose.* Too much of our activity is *ad hoc*, with too much emphasis on trivia.
2. *The Bureau staff is not pulling together.* We are more a collection of individuals than a team. . . . *A premium is placed on individual performance.* In combination, these factors tend to encourage uncoordinated, incomplete, and sometimes inaccurate Bureau staff work, lowered morale, and too much individual record building. *The Bureau, as an institution, cannot in the long run produce effectively under these conditions.*
3. *The staff doesn't get enough feedback* of information on *what* is wanted and *how* it is wanted.
4. *There is not a clear enough delegation from the Director's Office* on the issues and problems that should be handled at a lower level.
5. *The Bureau has serious personnel problems* which have not been resolved.
6. *Some members of the staff are overworked: others underworked.*
7. *The Bureau's internal and external instructions directly affects its workload and priorities. The role of the Offices in preparing them and assigning other work is ambivalent.* There are pitchers and umpires in the same game.[70]

What types of problems prompted these criticisms? Another working paper provided the following list of problems:

1. *Workload has expanded tremendously; staffing has not kept pace.*
   —We're overwhelmed by pieces of paper and crises.
   —*Much workload is externally imposed, e.g., greater demands by the White House.*
   —The examiners job has become a production job.
   —Results: lower quality, less familiarization with agencies' programs and substantive fields, family life suffers, *staff is called upon for judgements based on less and less program knowledge.*

95

2. We are performing functions which have outlived their usefulness, or could be performed somewhere else.
3. Three of the Bureau's five Offices were almost completely out of mainstream:
   —Office of Management and Organization
   —Office of Financial Management
   —Office of Statistical Standards
4. Bureau staff members stay on the same jobs too long.
5. *The Bureau does not possess enough of the skills needed to deal with today's problems.*
6. Some of our activities are irrational:
   —Employment ceilings are arbitrary in the extreme, yet we gather and "analyze" a raft of detail; OBR second-guesses the divisions without program knowledge (negotiating in a Byzantine marketplace" as expressed by one examiner).
   —Cutbacks are sometimes made with too little analysis.[71]

Similar interviews with agency and department personnel disclosed that the "prestige of the Bureau was at an all time low due to its inability to communicate the views of the President in a clear, timely, and authoritative manner, the excessive concentration on detail, and the lack of realism in the review process as a whole."[72]

The Bureau's internal organization had changed very little since the 1952 reorganization, despite the vastly changed environment in which it operated. The study group believed that the Bureau needed to recognize two types of flexibility in its general staff role: First, "flexibility to adjust to a changing world," which was not a Bureau hallmark and "flexibility to respond to changing Directors and Presidents." This role was "far more subtle to establish and nurture, and it presents the fundamental paradox of the permanent/personal staff."

"The Bureau was created to provide an institutional career staff to the Presidency. Its existence serves the President and the Director. Much of the latter's ultimate usefulness and power derive from the fact that he alone among White House Assistants has a large permanent staff with program knowledge and an institutional memory. With the growth of inter-agency and intergovernmental programs and problems these things are more important than ever.

"The paradox lies in the fact that permanency is the enemy of flexibility. The Bureau tradition of responding to changing Directors has not been equally honored by all parts of the Bureau in recent years. This has occurred at a time when the Director's style have demanded an increasingly personal staff relationship. Why did parts of the Bureau adjust more easily to the negativism of the Eisenhower years than to the activism of Kennedy and Johnson?"[73]

These observations created the possibility that the Bureau's career staff could not respond to the demands of an activist president. An administratively confidential paper on "The High Level Personnel Problem in the Bureau of the Budget" suggested that the "largest single problem" facing the Bureau was "serious personnel problems in the top career levels of the Bureau which have remained unsolved for years."[74] The paper noted that "problems cited in other papers, such as: the communication gulf between the Director and parts of the Bureau, unresponsiveness, and lack of coordination, have many of their roots in personnel and personality. Improved management of the Bureau, better organizational alignment, streamlined functions can all help meet these problems. Only personnel actions will solve some of them."

A report prepared by Merrill J. Collett, a consultant for the Bureau of the Budget, illustrated the severity of the Bureau's personnel problems. The report, based on personal and questionnaire interviews with a cross-section of Bureau staff concluded:

"Only at the first supervisory level (GS-16) does the Bureau represent to its staff a total institution, a cohesive organism of 500 dedicated public servants. Even at this level, all the top staff is concerned with program and not projects. No one is responsible for the internal management of the Bureau.

"Among the GS-13 through GS-15 group, the Bureau is not a coherent organization. . . . Among these professionals there is neither certainty nor unanimity as to who is running the shop."[75]

The Collett report was extremely critical in its assessment of staff mobility, arguing that

"Of 69 Supervisory level employees (GS-16 through 18), 68% have had 16 years or more of Bureau service and 60% have served in only two offices or divisions. Of 285 non-supervisory employees (GS-7 through 15), 60% have had five years or less of Bureau service and 73% have had 10 years or less—while 92% have served in only two divisions. . . .

"In spite of the caliber of the Bureau staff, however, some of its professionals are on the shelf. In response to an interview question concerning personal knowledge of Bureau professional staff who are not carrying their weight, answers from Grades 9 through 18 were distressingly prompt, and invariably indicated a thinking of some rather than one."[76]

Collett suggested that roughly 7 percent of the Bureau's program professionals were not doing their job, and the BOB was "not large enough to indulge itself in this manner, especially in view of its increasing work load." The report observed that

"Over the years the Bureau has been a kindly and compassionate employer. But true kindness demands keeping a professional on his toes by calling his attention to sub-standard work as it appears and following through to make sure that the work improves or the employee moves either to another trial or out. The reasons for sub-standard work may vary, from carelessness to senility, but when the reasons are established, action consistent with the facts must follow. Otherwise the entire work group—superiors, colleagues, and subordinates—become burdened as they adjust, absorb, or overlook the productive gap."[77]

The Bureau's "personnel problem" paper noted that the "inability to respond appears to be primarily a product of operating style, of becoming set in ones ways." Little career rotation and even less influx of new blood created a situation where the staff found it "difficult to respond responsibly." This personnel problem did not apply to "the incompetent or the has been," but rather to someone with five to seven years' experience in the same job. The BOB could not afford to retain an individual in a GS-16, 17, 18 job if that job was the capstone of a career, nor could an individual remain in the same Bureau job for more than ten years and retain the ability to be fully responsive to different Directors and Presidents. The report observed that it did not make sense that the same person occupied an important career position in a government policy area for twenty years. Likewise, the Bureau, close to the President and exposed, could not set an example of unwillingness or inability to deal promptly with serious personnel problems.[78]

The easiest solution would be counselling out at the appropriate time, but the evidence indicated that the appropriate time never came. The Budget Bureau was too small an organization to accommodate former Office and Division Chiefs, and these individuals would have no trouble finding a job outside the Bureau.[79]

The authors of the "personnel problem" paper favored establishing an agreed-upon tenure for Office and Division Chiefs, with a concomitant up-or-out policy for the GS-16s and 17s. Simply rotating Division Chiefs and other high level senior staff would not solve the problem. In short, "a fixed limited tenure for Office and Division Chiefs could benefit the individual and the Government. It would refresh the individual (or keep him from going stale) and thus greatly increase his contribution to government and society."[80]

The Bureau's personnel problems illustrate that long-time service in one agency (a basic tenet of the civil service system and of BOB's institutional knowledge) hindered the mobility and creativity of BOB professionals. Although Bureau officials provided institutional memory and continuity for the presidency, they had lost the ability to respond to disparate (in this case, activist) Directors and Presidents. Allen

99

Schick observed that "the Bureau's failure to orient itself to the service of the President was due largely to its institutional status. . . . An institutionalized Bureau could serve every President with fidelity, but it could effectively serve only a caretaker President. It could not be quick or responsive enough for an activist President who wants to keep a tight hold over program initiatives."[81]

The study group believed that the Director and Deputy Director were too preoccupied in their roles as presidential assistants to continue the charade that they could also give adequate attention to the Bureau's organization and management. Schick argued that "wearing his second hat the director pulled other Budget men into the frenzy of presidential policy-making, but this role laid bare one inadequacy of the Bureau and gave rise to another. It revealed the unpreparedness of the Bureau to serve as a presidential institution, and it barred the Director from giving adequate attention to the management of his own organization."[82] Someone had to be appointed general manager of the Bureau. The steering group believed that "because [the Director] depends on the Bureau (i.e., the staff) as much as it depends on him, every Director has a responsibility to preserve and nurture it, for the benefit of himself, his successor, the President, and the Presidency. It is not enough to use it, although this is vital, or to sing its praises, although this is useful. Like a forest, the Bureau must be managed if it is to continue to produce."[83]

One of the most disturbing consequences of the Budget Director's role as a White House Assistant was that the distinction between personal and institutional staff work in the Executive Office had become blurred for the Director as well as for the President. To the degree Bureau staff supported the Director in these ad hoc assignments, the distinction was also disintegrating for them. The Budget Director was in a double bind because his role as Special Assistant depended on his personal relationship with the President, but it also depended on the Director's institutional staff. One of the reasons Presidents relied on their Budget Directors was because other staff assistants did not have the perspective, the resources, the flow of knowledge, and the contacts offered by the Budget Director's institutional staff of 500 professionals. A Budget Director who gained entry into the President's inner circle, but neglected his institutional staff, ran the risk that somewhere down the road his staff would be unable to provide the Director with an institutional perspective. To compromise this institutional resource was to deny the President a government-wide perspective on emerging policy issues. There was general agreement among the steering group that "if we cannot find a means to tighten up the management of the Bureau's operation, we face a gradual deterioration of the Bureau's ability to perform its function adequately."[84]

On July 11, 1967 Joseph Califano wrote to President Johnson that "the [Heineman] proposals to strengthen the Executive Office of the President are clearly steps in the right direction. Schultze is carrying out his own study of BOB and I will be working closely with him, Heineman, and Kermit Gordon to develop a practical and workable plan to modernize BOB, so it can be an instrument of much greater power and use to you."[85] The 1967 self-study represents an important milestone or, more appropriately, tombstone in the BOB's history. As one working paper observed, "if significant change does not follow the evaluation phase, there is every reason to believe that a further decrease in Bureau effectiveness will ensue in the months ahead."[86]

The major purpose of the 1967 BOB self-study was to ascertain what the Budget Bureau "needed to do to serve the President better in the context of today's problems."[87] Several internal BOB changes were implemented. The Bureau's Office of Management and Organization was abolished and replaced by an Office of Executive Management (OEM) and placed under the direction of a statutory Assistant Director. The OEM was expected to focus on interagency and intergovernmental management problems. The seven examining divisions were reorganized into six units by consolidating related programs and agencies. (Appendix Two, E.) A Human Resources Program Division was established to cover under one roof the Great Society programs of HEW, HUD, Labor, and the Veterans Administration. A statutory assistant Director, William Carey, was assigned to this new Division. Roger Jones was assigned responsibility for assisting the Director in internal Bureau management, and a small Resource Planning staff and Program Evaluation staff were established under statutory assistant Directors.

The 1960s brought a marked increase in the level of White House staff activity in formulating legislation central to the President's program. As a consequence of the New Frontier and Great Society emphasis on new programs, policy-shaping initiatives progressively shifted from normal institutional channels, where proposals originating in the federal bureaucracy came "welling up" for BOB clearance, to direct intervention by White House emissaries, who short-circuited these slow and in their minds often unwieldly channels. These changes originated with John Kennedy's campaign pledge and inaugural speech promise to "get the country moving again," and reached legislative fulfillment in Lyndon Johnson's Great Society programs.

Between 1964 and 1968 the BOB was confronted by a problem in the magnitude of presidential staff work. In 1949, with a federal budget of $40 billion, the BOB had 534 employees; in 1969, with a $193 billion budget, the Bureau had 503 employees. The BOB of the 1960s assumed new responsibilities, special projects, rush assignments and added reporting burdens. Between 1963 and 1967, twenty-one new health plans, seventeen educational programs, fifteen economic programs, twelve urban development programs, four manpower training programs, and seventeen new research development programs were passed into law. Since 1962 the physical volume of correspondence signed by the Office of the Director increased 80 percent, the volume signed by the Director increased 100 percent.

Reaction time was very short. Problems arose and gave rise to uncertainties about whether the BOB was suited to expanded staff work. In addition, the Budget Bureau was held responsible for things it was not prepared to do. Developing new programs and providing operational coordination had previously been done on a selective basis "and only when there was no other logical place to make the assignment."[88] Arthur Maass long ago noted that the Budget Bureau was "institutionally incapable of positive policy formulation" because spending money ran counter to the BOB's orientation and "the permanent and career nature of the Budget Bureau tend[ed] to make the organization overly cautious and thus not well-suited for making or proposing political decisions on important matters of policy."[89] Moreover, the Bureau's institutional biases "inevitably caused conflict," Harold Seidman argued, "with activists on the White House staff mainly concerned with promoting the President's political interests."[90] William Carey reported that "the use of the Bureau of the Budget encountered problems of policy dichotomies, since the Budget Director was under explicit and colorful instructions from the President to hold expenditures below bare-bones totals, while the Califano staff was out to build the President's program in positive and politically profitable terms."[91] The Bureau's dependability proved to be its greatest liability. William Carey cogently noted that "the Bureau could have been just what its formal charter called for—a fiscal and management arm of the White House. As we know, it became much more than this, and it did so because: (a) Budget Directors believed that resource management equated with the shaping of public policy; (b) they consciously molded the Bureau as an all-purpose back-up staff to the President; and (c) Presidents liked the stamina and dependability of the Bureau and accepted the institution for what it was."[92]

By 1969, however, the Bureau of the Budget was a tired institution. A former senior official recalled that "the demands of the White House staff on us were ad hoc. . . . We were running in circles all of the time. We were consuming our capital at a tremendous rate and not replenishing it. The Bureau was playing the defense that was on the field all of the time and was old and it was slowing." How did the Budget Bureau become so vulnerable to external demands? Part of the answer was suggested in the 1967 self-study paper identifying the White House staff's inability to keep pace with the changing role of the presidency *and* the President's need for a point where loyalty was not divided.[93] The BOB survived the activism of the 1960s by serving as the receptacle for responsibilities not in accord with its traditional role and by coopting its institutional perspective. As Gary Bombardier noted, "the usefulness to the President of much of what the Bureau did was called into question as not being responsive to changes in the political system and in the role of the President within that system."[94] Much like an aging prize fighter who used all his years of ring experience simply to go the distance with a faster, younger fighter, the Budget Bureau gave it all in program formulation and operational activities. A new President, however, faced serious problems in managing federal programs, and the BOB was judged institutionally inadequate in the program development and management area.

The Office of Management and Budget:
A Change Rather than Progress, 1970-1979

During the 1968 presidential transition, President-elect Nixon established a fifteen-person transition task force chaired by Frank Lindsay, President of ITEK Corporation of Lexington, Massachusetts. The Lindsay Task Force recommended that "the President-elect give first priority to organizing more effectively the White House-Executive Office as the best way to improve the operations of the entire Executive Branch."[1] Nixon was advised to renew the recently expired Reorganization Act and to establish an Advisory Committee to study the organization of the Executive Branch. On March 27, 1969 Congress renewed the President's reorganization authority and on April 5, 1969 Nixon established the Advisory Council on Executive Organization chaired by Roy Ash of Litton Industries. The other Council members were John Connally, former Governor of Texas; Richard Paget, President of Cresap, McCormack and Paget; Fred Kappel, Chairman of the Executive Committee of AT&T; George Baker, Dean of the Harvard Graduate School of Business; and Walter Thayer, President of Whitney Industries and former publisher of the *Herald Tribune* (Thayer joined the Council on June 2, 1969).

When Roy Ash was selected to head the President's Advisory Council, President Nixon was already familiar with Ash's ideas on Executive Office organization. During the 1968 transition period Ash had prepared a ten-page memorandum for the President-elect on "Executive Office Organization," which recommended an Office of Executive Management (OEM). This OEM would encompass the BOB's budgetary responsibilities and add three new features: a

105

Division of Evaluation, a Domestic Policy Council (DPC), and a Division of Program Coordination. On the basis of this ten-page memo and diagram, Nixon instructed Ash to prepare his reorganization plan for implementation.[2]

Nevertheless, the Ash plan was dropped when the incoming administration, facing an opposition Congress, learned that Congressional approval would be necessary to implement the plan. President Nixon's first Budget Director, and as it transpired the last BOB Director, Robert Mayo, was never told of the plan for OEM because it was feared that the Budget Director would utilize the BOB's resources against the plan if he realized that his organization might one day be subsumed under an OEM. President Nixon asked Ash to be his first Budget Director, but Ash declined. Mayo accepted the Budget Directorship without the knowledge that a Director of OEM might one day be placed over him.

For several months the staff of the Ash Council reviewed all previous reform proposals for the Executive Office, interviewed over two hundred people, including two former Budget Directors, former and present Cabinet officers, and former President Johnson. On August 20, 1969, the Council forwarded its first recommendation to President Nixon, agreeing with the problems identified in the Heineman and Lindsay reports, and recommending the creation of an Office of Executive Management (OEM) to assist the President in managing the federal government, and a Domestic Policy Council (DPC) to provide "a place where major domestic programs may be evaluated against each other·and against available resources, and integrated for maximum effectiveness."[3]

President Nixon requested that the Council be more specific, and two months later the Council forwarded a revised set of recommendations to the President. The Council's selling point was that the OEM and DPC represented "the first major improvement in the President's management capability since the Brownlow Commission recommendations were implemented by President Roosevelt in 1939."[4]

106

The Domestic Policy Council (DPC), later changed to the Domestic Council (primarily because John Ehrlichman thought that policy was too restrictive a term), was described as an office where the total range of domestic policy could be coordinated and developed. The DPC would make forecasts, synthesize policy alternatives, provide rapid response to presidential emergencies, and constantly revise ongoing programs. The DPC would be the key link between the President and the agencies by communicating presidential goals and philosophy to the agencies and providing the President with agency positions.

The Office of Executive Management (OEM) was envisioned as the President's chief management arm, institutionalizing budget and program evaluation, program coordination, legislative clearance, executive personnel development, and organization and management systems improvement. The report emphasized that OEM was not simply the renaming of BOB, but rather, a "fundamental departure and innovation." OEM would be result-oriented and "embody a concept of management that goes well beyond the present emphasis on budget. . . . A substantially different orientation to the President's managerial job will emerge."[5]

OEM incorporated several important changes: (1) presidential appointees would head the President's institutional staff in the management area, thus ensuring better responsiveness to presidential priorities; (2) OEM would focus on crucial management functions such as program coordination, executive personnel, organizational and management processes, and information systems; (3) OEM would give the President a staff commensurate with the scope of his management problems; (4) by consciously emphasizing management rather than budget, OEM would "create a climate more conducive to managerial effectiveness"; and (5) executive personnel programs would finally receive the attention they deserved.

The Ash Council believed that their recommendations represented "a modern response to the growing complexity of

107

government tasks."[6] The President would now have the tools to delegate responsibilities to the agencies and to decentralize operations at the state and local levels. President Nixon agreed with the October recommendations and requested the Council to prepare the necessary legislation. On March 12, 1970 President Nixon forwarded Reorganization Plan No. 2 to Congress.

The proposed plan would replace the BOB with a new Office of Management and Budget and establish a Domestic Council. The name OEM was replaced at a late stage in the Council's preparation, first to the Office of Management, then to OMB when congressional leaders opposed the dropping of "Budget." The President's reorganization message argued that "the Domestic Council will be primarily concerned with what we do; the Office of Management and Budget will be primarily concerned with how we do it, and how well we do it. . . . The creation of the Office of Management and Budget represents far more than a mere change of name for the Bureau of the Budget. It represents a basic change in concept and emphasis, reflecting the broader management needs of the Office of the President."[7]

The top career staff of the Budget Bureau openly opposed the Ash Council recommendations for an OEM. According to Roy Ash, "one of the biggest problems in trying to convert the Bureau of the Budget to the Office of Management and Budget was that the pocket of greatest resistance, of political resistance, was the Bureau of the Budget. Some of those guys went up to the Hill to sabotage that thing, and to really turn the screws up on some of them. That was the biggest resistance block right there."[8] Members of the Ash Council found that BOB was a formidable adversary. When Budget Director Mayo briefed his top staff, he described the Ash recommendations as a "plan which would modernize the title of the BOB." Following the briefing, the staff "reacted angrily and the general sense of the meeting was "who the hell does the Ash Council think it is. . . ?" The officers were determined to block the plan.[9]

Mayo's reservations included the omission of the OEM Director from the DPC; the Ash Council's belief that budget-making could be separated from policy-making; the participation of DPC staff in the Budget Director's internal review of agency budget requests; and Congressional objections to the delegation of all BOB functions to the President, who would then delegate them to the Director of OEM. Most of these were routine administrative functions (travel regulations, approval of property transfers) that belonged with the Director of OEM, not the President.[10]

In a conversation with Mayo, Ash "observed that BOB has many ways at its disposal to kill the plan and asked Mayo's assurance that neither he nor his people would sabotage the plan through extra-legal channels."[11] The Bureau, however, resorted to subtle defense procedures to offset the Ash proposals. First, came an announcement that James Frey would be appointed to fill the long-vacant post of Executive Assistant Director. Frey would direct the internal management processes of the Bureau's work and develop improved communications within the Bureau. Following the Frey appointment, a member of the Ash Council observed that "the Bureau had filled this post several times in its fifty-year history—each time when it was under attack." Richard Tanner Johnson noted that "Frey's appointment . . . marked a significant defensive move . . . by devoting the full-time efforts of one of its able and respected professionals, the Bureau had been able to anticipate criticism and institute changes before they were imposed from the outside."[12]

The Bureau revealed another defense mechanism by misplacing the Ash Council's additional million-dollar budget request for fiscal year 1971 until it could not be incorporated into the President's Special Fund Budget. "The BOB was thus forcing the Council to make a special line-item request to the Congressional Committee. Such a request was vulnerable to Congressional veto."[13]

On May 5, the House Subcommittee on Executive and Legislative Reorganization reported a resolution of disapproval on Reorganization Plan No. 2, leaving the Ash Council shocked. The House Subcommittee objected to the ambiguity in the plan's language and the latitude for presidential interpretation and action. The technical objections, however, covered more deep-seated suspicion of the White House staff and the fact that the Director of the Domestic Council would not be required to testify before Congress.

On May 7, the Senate Subcommittee on Executive Reorganization began hearings on the Reorganization bill. Chairman Ribicoff, a strong supporter of the Reorganization plan as it stood, was intent on saving the President's plan from the House resolution. At the Senate hearings Ribicoff charged that the Budget Bureau had been totally unresponsive to the problems of Presidents Kennedy, Johnson, and Nixon.

"The most frustrating agency in the government is the Bureau of the Budget. . . . I think that the most backward bureaucracy in the Federal Government is the Bureau of the Budget. Nothing moves when it gets there. They stalemate. They are people without imagination. And they frustrate the work of members of the Cabinet. . . .

"I have not found in the past 10 years any imagination and understanding [in BOB] of the great problems sweeping this nation and I cannot see where the Budget Bureau has really been a help to either President Kennedy, President Johnson or President Nixon in many of the great domestic problems that we have."[14]

As a former Cabinet official, Ribicoff was not an impartial observer. At one point, Congressman Holifield (a witness at the Senate hearings) interrupted Ribicoff to defend the BOB. Ribicoff had been arguing that the President needed a Domestic Council so that Cabinet officers would "have somebody in the White House working with him on domestic programs and not bucking it up to a bureaucracy in the Bureau of the Budget to find it dies or it is emasculated." Holifield interjected that he also wanted to help the President, but it was important that Ribicoff understand that Congress shared the blame for not authorizing BOB personnel increases: "In 1950, the budget was in round numbers $43 billion. In 20 years, it has gone to $197 billion, almost a five-time increase. Yet the personnel of the Bureau of the Budget has only been increased from 531 to 553—by 22 people. Now, within that number that I have just quoted, 46 were in the Management Division of the Bureau of the Budget in 1950 and 49 today."[15]

Ribicoff remained steadfast in his fight to ensure passage of the reorganization plan. He noted that the Budget Bureau staff were "jealous of their functions and their power [and] the happiest group in the Government today will be the Bureau of the Budget by the rejection of this plan, because this gives the Bureau of the Budget a chance to keep playing one element of the Government against the other or keep their power. *The Bureau of the Budget has become power hungry and power crazy. This is an opportunity to take away some of the function of the Budget Bureau and put it in the Office of the Presidency, where it belongs.*"[16] What prompted Ribicoff's charge that BOB had become power-hungry and crazy? Why would the Budget Bureau enjoy playing one element against the other? After all, BOB always said "no" for the President, but by 1970 there was general frustration with the inability of institutional machinery to solve administrative problems.

There was certainly no lack of diversity in opinion on what the reorganization plan represented. To Hugh Heclo the "change from BOB to OMB expressed a legitimate concern for the political responsibility and responsiveness of the people making important decisions."[17] To Allen Schick the reorganization was a culmination of recent developments that pointed to "a slippage in the perceived ability of the Bureau to discharge the functions it had acquired over the past half-century."[18] To William Carey "the thesis of Plan No. 2 seems to be that the managerial dimensions of the modern presidency have become so magnified and strategic

111

that the Bureau should now concentrate its efforts there and divest itself of its pretensions to the shaping of public policy."[19] To Roy Ash reorganization was a way to improve EOP management processes, *and* to break up the BOB. "There was a lore that surrounded that old Bureau of the Budget and we deliberately tried to break it. One of the reasons for changing the name was to break the lore. The lore was that you had to be very anonymous, way back in the woodwork . . . doing things in an unchanging way, a narrow perception, even narrower than the 1921 Act. They had a nice comfortable spot down there with a degree of expertise that helped to protect the institution."[20]

Nevertheless, with the House Subcommittee's recommendation for disapproval, the odds were not favorable that the reorganization plan would be approved by a vote of the full House. The Ash Council initiated a massive lobbying effort to gain passage for their plan. The Council staff sought to generate favorable editorials and news columns. House Minority Leader Gerald Ford was informed that the President expected maximum Republican loyalty on the floor vote, and supporting letters were mailed to all members of the House. The Council staff assisted the minority staff of the House Government Operations Committee in drafting its report accompanying the resolution of disapproval and Council members tried to talk with all Democrats known to be voting against the plan.

The strategy worked, because on May 13, 1970 the House voted 164 for and 193 against the disapproval resolution. On July 1, 1970 the Bureau of the Budget was redesignated the Office of Management and Budget. Executive Order 11541 delegated to the OMB Director all functions formerly assigned to the BOB by law and vested in the President by Reorganization Plan No. 2, and all functions formerly assigned to the BOB by Executive Order or administrative action. On August 7 OMB Director George Shultz imparted a noble charter on the OMB when he announced that "the Office of Management and Budget will be in a position to implement the President's desire for strong, effective, and responsive management. . . . The new emphasis on management and the newly created management divisions will provide the basis for more effective program coordination and evaluation. The public and the President will be better served."[21]

The Ash Council succeeded because the Bureau's popularity with Congress was at an all-time low, and many Congressmen believed that institutional changes were required. The BOB could never win a popularity contest with Congress, and the Council portrayed the Bureau as an unresponsive policy-making institution that needed to be curbed. In addition, the demands of the 1960s revealed the institutional weaknesses of a particular Presidential staff. First, the BOB's management arm proved unable to ameliorate the many intergovernmental problems facing both President and country; second, in order to service a legislatively activist President, the Bureau traded its long-run institutional perspective for short-term influence as the peddler of task force reports and unrealistic budget predictions. Moreover, over time (beginning in the Eisenhower years) the BOB career staff had rigidified. Presidential expectations surpassed Bureau capabilities and no one could turn off external demands.

The 1970 reorganization provided the President with increased institutional staff capability in program evaluation and coordination, government organization, information and management systems, and the development of executive talent. Yet, the dividing of government into two interests— the Domestic Council (what) and OMB (how and how well)—assumed that policy could be separated from administration. By 1977 only three percent of OMB professionals believed that the reorganization plan had worked as planned. These changes, however, did not significantly improve OMB's management role and raised the long-debated possibility that "M" did not belong in a budgeting office. (Appendix Two, F.)

In October 1971, for example, OMB sponsored a Federal

Management Improvement Conference, attended by over 300 managers from 34 departments and agencies in the federal government. Of the conferees who attended panels on OMB, 59 percent observed no significant changes in OMB compared to BOB, and only 35 percent believed that OMB gave more emphasis to management issues than did BOB. Only 17 percent of the conferees believed that OMB was more effective than its predecessor agency, and 65 percent recommended strengthening the management functions of OMB.[22]

A sub-panel on the "Impact of the New Management Emphasis on the Program Divisions and the Budget Process" concluded that little progress had been made on the budget-examining process as a result of the OMB's new emphasis on management. There was little change in the examiner's approach to reviewing program budgets, and examiners appeared confused about improving management through the budget process. No systematic communication existed between the budget and management functions, and OMB had not defined for the agencies what it meant by "management."

The sub-panel recommended that OMB recognize "the necessity for thinking through the meaning of the word management, and promulgating a series of specific objectives to Federal agencies." The sub-panel asked "whether the OMB's distinction between 'management' and 'budget' was the appropriate division on which to base its organization,"[23] and recommended that OMB consider organizing along lines of immediate, near-term and long-term analysis of presidential interests. It was clear to these federal managers that OMB had made only marginal gains in the management area in the fifteen months since Reorganization Plan No. 2 of 1970 was implemented.

Well over 50 percent of my survey respondents gave OMB a "fair" to "poor" rating when asked to evaluate the agency's management performance. When ranking the actual emphasis accorded budgeting and management in the day-to-day work of OMB, 86 percent of the respondents gave budgeting a "High Priority," compared to 14 percent response to a similar question for management. One OMB professional wrote that OMB lacked "a coherent strategy about management and what the President's role and its own role in management should be." Another respondent complained that "the management side suffers from a lack of direction and sense of purpose. Its structure is fragmented with several units involved in the same or similar functions . . . the Management by Objective initiative is virtually dead." Another respondent asked "is OMB really the place to have management responsibility?"

The 1976 National Academy of Public Administration transition recommendations also cited the "deterioration of the managerial role of OMB," as one of the most serious problems facing the President. The NAPA group reported that the "existing lack of an effective staff arm to the President for stimulating management improvement in the agencies and for developing further means of meeting problems common to groups of agencies is one of the most serious issues needing quick resolution by the President."[24] The management side of OMB lacked direction, charter, confidence, leadership, and purpose.

Nevertheless, a majority of NAPA participants favored retaining the "M" in OMB, but *only* if the Director and Deputy Director visibly supported management responsibilities as *an equal* to budgeting and legislative clearance. A minority of the NAPA group contended that "more than 50 years experience with BOB and OMB is enough to demonstrate that only in rare occasions can management thrive in the same institution as the budget function . . . [and] the increasing complexity of economic issues and the wider range of budget issues will make these occasions even rarer in the future."[25] This group recommended a new Executive Office unit incorporating the management responsibilities of OMB (including the Office of Federal Procurement Policy), and personnel management policy functions of the Government Services Administration.

115

Reorganization Plan No. 2 was also intended as the legitimate response to a vastly changed political environment in which the old Bureau of the Budget operated. By 1973, however, its successor's credibility as a presidential staff office was perhaps forever tarnished. OMB's institutional quandry developed, in part, from its very responsiveness to the political and stylistic needs of Richard Nixon. In 1970, for example, Nixon replaced his first Budget Director Robert Mayo with Secretary of Labor, George Shultz. Shultz was the first BOB or OMB Director to be assigned a White House Office and within a few months became President Nixon's trusted economic advisor (institutionalizing the 1960 trend of Budget Director qua Special Assistant). Shultz chaired a daily 7:30 a.m. White House staff meeting, attended an 8:00 a.m. select White House meeting, and a 3:00 p.m. meeting with Ehrlichman and the President.

More than a year following the creation of OMB, Dom Bonafede wrote in *The National Journal* that George Shultz had "established himself as Mr. Nixon's principal advisor in domestic affairs. Working with handpicked aides, he has modified the original concept of the [OMB] as a purely policy-implementing agency by assuming some policy-making functions as well."[26] John Osborne wrote that "having fitted his principal assistants into neat organizational boxes . . . Nixon is forever jerking them out of their assigned roles and giving them several jobs. . . . George P. Shultz, the Director of the new Office of Management and Budget, counts himself lucky when he is able to sit through a weekly meeting of that agency's enlarged executive staff without being summoned to the President's office for consultation on matters that range from budgetary policy to school desegregation."[27] Osborne added that the most "interesting paradox" of Reorganization Plan No. 2 was that "Ehrlichman is deep in operation, Shultz in policy-making," the reverse of the Ash Council's recommendation that the Domestic Council deal with abstract problems of social programs, not management.

116

Shultz's relocation from the old Executive Office building to a second-floor White House location was predicated on the bureaucratic adage: "Proximity is power." Shultz believed that being "one-eardrum" away from the President was better than being across the street, and, with Nixon, it was better to be inside than outside the fence.

A major symbolic consideration was involved in the Director's relocation. Is it the quality of a working relationship or physical proximity that is most important? (If a Budget Director has access, it should not matter if he is fifteen blocks, fifteen feet, or fifteen seconds from the President.) Shultz obviously believed that, in his case, physical proximity would help to determine the quality of his working relationship. In addition, and despite Shultz's best intentions, the administration's span of political control over OMB was increased by the Director's location in the White House. While an OMB Director in the White House might add prestige for OMB, it merely institutionalizes the Director's role as a White House Special Assistant, and the distinction between personal and institutional staff responsibilities becomes even more blurred. Roger Jones argues, for example, that the head of institutional machinery cannot operate successfully from within the White House fence because "the virus of the environment and the availability to all kinds of things that don't have a thing to do with the institutional responsibilities, simply cannot thrive and flourish in that atmosphere."[28] Such was the decision of the 1960s when BOB Directors served as White House Special Assistants sans the office. Shultz's relocation simply institutionalized the relationship. In Shultz's case, however, "everybody in the White House felt they had a call on his services and they tried to use him in all kinds of ways that weren't really pertinent to what the hell he was supposed to be doing."[29]

Over 50 percent of my 1977 survey respondents who believed that the location of the Director's Office made a difference favored on OMB location to a White House office. Most of the open-ended responses emphasized the impor-

117

tance of the troops' seeing their Director as an institutional linkage between OMB and the White House.

The Director's location was perhaps the least of OMB's problems. Moreover, OMB was viewed by the Nixon administration as neither staffed by individuals known to be loyal to the President nor effectively oriented towards the political-policy role. Non-career Assistant Directors (Pads) were placed in charge of OMB's program divisions, replacing the traditional careerist leadership. The Pads have line rather than staff responsibilities for supervising OMB's program divisions, which deal directly with the agencies on all program and operational matters. Career division chiefs maintain responsibility for the day-to-day activities of their division, but now report to the Deputy Director through a non-career official. Important program decisions that once benefited from OMB's institutional memory are now made by the Pads. Wilfred Rommel, Assistant Director for Legislative Reference, explained that "if there is a policy issue now, it goes to a policy officer, not a career person." Another OMB official noted, "we bureaucrats no longer talk to the other bureaucrats about the budget—that's all handled by the political people."[30] Bert Lance added a new layer of two Executive Associate Directors to management and budget sides of OMB. The careerist is now separated from the Director by another level of political appointees.

Critics charge that the Pads are too political, possess too little program knowledge, remain in OMB too short a time to obtain that program knowledge, do not trust careerists, and, by handling the political interface which the Director used to handle, have eroded the independence of division chiefs and the decision-role of the Director. For example, one of the major conclusions of the 1976 NAPA transition report was that "the OMB staff's professional judgement on how best to achieve Presidential objectives has been seriously politicized through the political overlay at the Associate Director level. This politicizing effect should be eliminated."[31] Louis Fisher observed that the Pads "resulted in delays, frustration, and poor communication. Knowledgeable staffers with 'institutional memory' could not inform new policymakers that, for example, the 'square wheel' they thought to be a remarkable innovation had been tried twice before and found wanting, and why it had failed."[32] Wayne, Cole, and Hyde reported that under the Pads, "OMB's advisory mechanism seemed to be more sensitive to political factors and, conversely, less oriented toward making its recommendations on the substantive merits of the legislation."[33] Over 50 percent of my OMB respondents expressing an opinion on this issue believed that the Pads downgraded the contribution made by career officials in OMB. Most open-ended responses cited the cutting off of channels to the agencies *and* Director's Office.

Nevertheless, subtle distinctions exist between the charge that the Pads politicized OMB in a narrow partisan sense, and that an attempt was made to increase the political sensitivity of career staff through the imposition of non-career officials into OMB's key decision slots. Part of the Pads' credibility problem evolved by their being caught in the middle of the administration's responsiveness program. A March 17, 1972 memo from OMB's soon-to-be Deputy Director, Fred Malek on the subject of "Increasing the Responsiveness of the Executive Branch" identified OMB Assistant Director William Gifford (a Pad) as the administration's key contact "for operating matters with the Departments." Malek expected Gifford to ensure that politically sensitive grants received special consideration, with OMB communicating the administration's "political priorities as well as the 'must' operating decisions" to the Departments.[34] OMB came away from the Watergate revelations stigmatized as a political honcho—the administration's equivalent of Atilla the Hun. The Pads were guilty by association—identified in the Malek memo as the political pressure point for the responsiveness program. As a result, the Pads have been labelled "bad guys," and their proper role has been glossed over when deciding what kinds of political analysis should

119

be made, by whom, and how it should be cranked into the decision-making process.

The idea of statutory Assistant Directors was not a new one for OMB. The BOB always maintained a few non-career officials and in 1959 a minority of the BOB self-study group favored additional Assistant Directors for staff assignments in specific program areas. The study group warned, however, that "assignments to such assistants must not be allowed to obscure the direct line of direction and reporting between the Director/Deputy Director team and the Office and Division heads."[35]

The 1959 report did not anticipate that events of the 1960s would force the BOB to shift its internal emphasis from budget to program review, revealing as an Achilles heel the staff's non-political professionalism. By 1967, another BOB self-study group found that a "general complaint about the Bureau staff is that, while the examiners are generally knowledgeable about their programs, they do not have 'a point of view' . . . examiners tend to come up with several alternatives for presentation without any recommendation as to which is the best alternative."[36] The same paper provided comments from agency officials interviewed during the 1967 study: "The Bureau lacks political people. . . . The Bureau is almost completely without people who have political sensitivity and who read the signals. . . . The Bureau staff is often naive politically and persists doggedly on a completely unrealistic point." Nevertheless, the working paper concluded that "the Bureau will probably have to live with the complaint that it is often politically naive. For if the Bureau is to evaluate and recommend 'the best' of several alternatives, it is unrealistic to expect that this 'best' alternative will always be most feasible. But just because the Bureau is looked to for objective evaluation, there is no reason its staff should lack political sensitivity."[37]

The 1967 study group recognized that the President did not need an OMB which put its head in the sand with respect to political factors in the name of objectivity and neutrality. Rather, a career staff needed to advise their superiors of all possible political considerations in which they were inadequately aware, and then let their politically appointed superiors make the decision.

The possibility for objective analysis may actually be increased by explicitly recognizing the Pads as a source of political knowhow, distinct from the careerists view. The problem is that the Pads have been too inexperienced in politics and have attempted several lame efforts to politicize decisions in the name of undefined management responsibilities. Fifty-three percent of my OMB respondents believed that *since 1970* OMB had become more politicized but less objective in its work. The Pads, removed from the line of command, could work on ad hoc problems as part of the Director's immediate staff. Important contributions could be made in analyses of complex issues that cut across the functions of departments in the government and divisions of OMB, day-to-day liaison with Congress, and especially sensitive operational problems.

The most crushing blow to OMB's credibility came during the Watergate period. In the last months of the Nixon administration, with the President's attention focused primarily on legal matters, responsibility for running the government literally fell to OMB and Nixon loyalist Roy Ash. There was a grim comedy to the sequence that brought OMB to its powerful Watergate position. "Who would have guessed," Aaron Wildavsky noted, "that President Nixon (via the Watergate affair) would play Ten Little Indians with the White House Staff: The Office of Management and Budget regained power because it survived. *Apres moi the OMB.*"[38] At the peak of Watergate, journalist John Herbers reported that "in many respects (OMB) has become a surrogate President, administering the Nixon policies as its top officials see them."[39] Richard Nathan reported that "the Office of Management and Budget played a stronger role in this period, with the President and his top White House aides increasingly preoccupied by Watergate and attendent problems."[40]

The work to be done involved controlling the day-to-day

operations of the domestic bureaucracy and, in effect, making decisions that should have been made by Cabinet or agency officials. With John Ehrlichman and several members of the Domestic Council staff either under investigation or indicted, OMB moved into the role vacated by the Domestic Council. In particular, Ash, Deputy Director Malek, and the four Associate Directors (Pads) replaced the Domestic Council as the critical link between agency heads and the White House. According to Ash, "after Ehrlichman left, it was downhill sailing all the way. OMB clearly and undisputably became a presidential right hand. It was absolutely a myth to say that the government was not managed in the last few months of the Nixon administration. It was probably better managed in terms of government function than it has been in any other time in American history, except not by the President. We had that place humming. The agencies weren't necessarily happy with it because they were all subordinate to us, but we had that place humming."[41]

The precise meaning of "humming" and the depth of OMB's surrogate role are disputed. Former OMB Deputy Director Paul O'Neil suggests that the major problems were stylistic. Cabinet officers "felt they didn't have an opportunity to sit down and tell the President personally what was on their minds. If it appeared to agency heads that OMB was intervening between them and the President, it was only because Nixon did not want to deal with the agency heads themselves. Rather than blame the President, they blamed OMB."[42] Roy Ash's first advice to President Ford followed a similar track: "I told him that he should be doing what I was doing. I told him to go out and speak to the agency heads. You the President should do it."[43] A former BOB/OMB official informed me that while Ash's perspective connoted effective operation, "the humming was quite of a different source and intent. Management was concerned with trivia, not basic function. Telling agencies how to do unimportant things was not management, and neither was an attempt to bite them with the President's teeth or larger issues.

122

. . . OMB tried to fill a political vacuum, but agencies, by and large, simply hunkered down and either gave mere lip service or delayed decisions on OMB ultimata until after Ford took over. By then OMB was so cordially hated that Ford's reorganization folks wanted to clip OMB's wings."

Congressional hearings for passage of confirmation requirements for the OMB Director and Deputy Director[44] illustrate Congressional perceptions of non-neutral OMB. Chairman Chet Holifield began the hearings by noting that "the OMB is not some mystical or magic instrument reserved exclusively for Presidential use. . . . The President seems to have lost sight of this fact in his impounding actions. . . . As I see it, the larger issue at stake is the prerogative of the Congress, its power and prestige as an institution." Representative Wright observed that "the people who comprise the Office of Management and Budget are slide-rule experts and people who know the price of everything but the value of nothing. . . . They sit there with this enormous power, wielding an ax or scalpel over the prostrated body politic, which is lying there being operated upon—sometimes not even knowing the identity of its surgeon." Congressman John Melcher called OMB a "veritable elephant among the mice" that "goes its way beholden to nobody but the President. . . . I want to make it clear that I believe it is time to put a jerk line on the OMB Director and that includes the present Director, Roy Ash, [but] only after he promises to bring his agency into cooperation with the Congress instead of running it like a Frankenstein monster." Representative Alexander charged that "this nation cannot afford to allow a miniscule group of elitists who believe they know what's good for the people . . . to dictate the shape and direction of the future." Representative J. J. Pickle argued that OMB had become "the invisible Government of the United States" and that "OMB may unintentionally be threatening our constitutional concept of public government." Senator Ervin argued that "the OMB has developed into a major governmental agency with enormous policymaking and operational functions, responsibilities, and authority. It has become a Super Cabinet agency."

In 1973 Congress took steps to diminish the chances that an OMB Director could keep Congress uninformed on budgetary decisions. Legislation was passed requiring Senate confirmation for both the OMB Director and Deputy Director. The Senate voted 64-17 for confirmation retroactive to Ash and Malek, but the President vetoed the proposal. (Congress redrafted the bill to make it apply to future OMB Directors and Deputy Directors.) Fifty-six percent of my respondents favored confirmation for the OMB Director and Deputy Director. Most open-ended responses were similar: "Yes, in order to screen out persons like Roy Ash and Fred Malek." "As OMB is now very political, and no longer a staff office, confirmation is proper; this was not true of BOB." "Yes, it solidifies the increasing politicization of OMB."

What have all these changes meant to OMB's standing in the EOP? On June 23, 1970 the National Academy of Public Administration held a colloquium on Reorganization Plan No. 2, during which William Carey cogently remarked that, "in the end, the question will not be whether the Domestic Council or the OMB did well or poorly, but whether the aggregate leadership and performance of the presidency meets expectations of quality, sensitivity, and decisiveness."[45] By 1973, impoundments, Watergate, excessive abuse of executive privilege, and a siege psychology in the White House left little doubt that the presidency failed to meet such leadership expectations. Under Ehrlichman's leadership, for example, the Domestic Council never became operational in planning macro-policy, and "evolved instead into a transmission belt for daily policy decisions to and from the President and a political management organization that handled whatever problem the moment dictated."[46] On the other hand, OMB's choice was to be the President's controller or just another unit controlled by the White House. OMB was perceived as a "Frankenstein monster," because its job was to help the President accomplish *his* mission. As visibility grew, outsiders could "no longer distinguish between OMB's governmental authority as an institution of the Presidency and its political power as the President's personal staff."[47] This was nowhere more evident than when Elliot Richardson became Attorney General and instructed his staff not to deal with either the White House staff *or* OMB.

The Office of Management and Budget was a major casualty of the Nixon presidency, in part for what it did, but also for what it appeared to be doing. By responding to the partisan needs of the President, OMB depleted valuable credibility with its other clients—leading many observers to maintain that OMB could not serve the long-range needs of the presidency. Because the Nixon administration had little use for neutrality sans partisanship, OMB's government-wide perspective was utilized for exerting political leverage over the executive establishment.

The final blow came when President Ford's transition team singled out OMB for playing too dominant a role during the Watergate period and recommended that OMB's powers be curtailed. Thus OMB paid a price for its responsiveness to Nixon's goals. Its capacity to serve the President as an impartial, professional career staff was greatly compromised when its cloak of anonymity was lifted. Since then, OMB has had to divert many staff hours into justifying its work to the public and the press. The net result was that many Washington observers perceived the need to rethink OMB's raison d'être in the EOP. A 1976 NAPA report prepared for the Senate Select Committee on Presidential Campaign Activities was adamant in its observation that "in any effort to restore the staff role to the Executive Office of the President, the Office of Management and Budget must receive particular attention."[48] The next chapter focuses on the present and future of a presidential staff agency.

The Future of the Office of Management and Budget: An Institutional Dilemma

> "One of the problems of institutions is that people keep trying to relive the past and it is not now possible for the Bureau to again go back. The last decade made that impossible and the question is where do you go from here."
> —*Observations of a former BOB/OMB official, 1976*

> "The mission of the Office of Management and Budget is to function as an objective staff agency to the President."
> —*Former OMB Director Bert Lance, 1977*

> "I think OMB is going to be as strong as it ever was."
> —*OMB Director James T. McIntyre, Jr., 1978*

By utilizing OMB as a partisan agent in the Executive Branch, President Nixon impaired OMB's vital contribution to the presidency and raised several questions on what role this staff unit should play in the federal system. As Hugh Heclo observed, the "changing norms and relationships [in OMB] call into question the possibility of preserving the institution as a source of impartial continuity for the presidency."[1] While 89 percent of OMB professionals surveyed believed their institution still maintained a "favorable" reputation with the President, only 29 percent believed OMB maintained a favorable reputation with the Departments and agencies, and only 19 percent responded similarly for OMB's post-Watergate reputation with Congress. In 1970, OMB was strategically given more political clout so that it could increase its partisan involvement in administrative policy-making. The easiest way for an organization to become politicized is to become identified as the spokesperson for a given political issue. The Pads, relocation of the Director's office to the White House, the responsiveness program, impoundment battles, and Watergate provided the groundwork for such perceptions.

OMB's dilemma is that its effectiveness depends upon responsiveness to presidential needs, and Presidents must decide whether they want a partisan agent or a politically sensitive budget/management staff. More often than not, however, OMB has been viewed as politically naive and *then* made politically responsive through partisan means. The Nixon years revealed the shortcomings of a too responsive OMB when utilized for noninstitutional purposes. As Heclo noted, "[OMB's] choice is to be of use to the President of the day or to atrophy. OMB preferred to be of use."[2] The institutional effects of OMB's responsiveness were obvious to President Ford's 1974 transition team, which reported that OMB had become "too involved in departmental processes and [was] limiting the department's ability to come up with innovative ideas."[3] Transition team workers believed that OMB "had become an advocate of policy rather than a politically neutral analytic tool" and that OMB "was imposing budgetary decisions on other Federal departments and agencies that were based on political considerations rather than the economic program approved by Congress."[4] The 1976 NAPA group concluded their transition recommendations to President Ford with a firm warning that "to the extent any politicizing effects of the Nixon White House remain, these should be promptly eliminated."[5] Yet when responding to a direct question on the Ford transition team recommendations, only 24 percent of OMB professionals agreed that OMB had been "too involved in agency policy-making," but over 60 percent of the OMB respondents believed that, *since 1970*, OMB had become more involved in the policy-making process.

The brief Ford presidency provided OMB, as with most of the discredited presidency, a chance to start anew. Ford soon replaced Nixon's Ash with James Lynn, the first OMB

Director to face Congressional confirmation.[6] Lynn did much to remove the taint of politicization, not by curbing OMB's powers, but rather by talking softly and assuring OMB's clients that the days of Frankenstein were over. To symbolize his sincerity, Lynn gave up his predecessor's White House office and moved back to the old Executive Office building. In addition, Lynn and his Associate Directors spent many hours on Capitol Hill explaining OMB budget decisions. Interestingly, only twelve months after the Ford transition recommendations, Joel Havemann reported that "nearly a year after President Ford's advisor's told him that the policy role of the Office of Management and Budget should be reduced, OMB still is the same powerful office established by Richard Nixon to coordinate policy for the President."[7] Havemann quoted Lynn as saying, "I have not been told by anybody the role of OMB is different than before."

President Carter has increased the number of political appointees in OMB, but has relied heavily on the office in budgeting and government reorganization. Carter views OMB as a "broad-gauged, highly professional institutionalized staff"[8] and assigned OMB responsibility for undertaking a major study of Executive Office management processes. The OMB reorganization study[9] focused on ways of improving and streamlining advisory, decision-making, coordinating, and administrative support functions in the EOP, and minimizing duplication and overlap of missions. Such administrative studies may be the most optimal "M" role for OMB and certainly comes closer than any definition of the last decade to what the Brownlow Committee envisioned when it designated the BOB as the President's key management staff in the EOP.

While the Bert Lance episode did little to improve OMB's *public* image, insiders never charged Lance with incompetence as OMB Director. Lance followed Lynn's lead during his confirmation hearings and assured everyone that "OMB should not be trying to run the government through the Executive Office, but should provide constructive coordination where required, and where the President wishes."[10] Lance, in fact, was probably the most influential in a long line of BOB/OMB Directors qua Special Assistants. His critics argued that Lance did not pay enough attention to OMB's internal organization and was not familiar with budgetary details. Nevertheless, during budget presentations to President Carter, Lance gave senior careerists the opportunity to explain decisions directly to the President (while Lance sat at the President's side of the table).[11]

Lance's successor, James McIntyre, is in a catch-22 situation. The demands on OMB have never been greater, at a time when OMB's power vis-à-vis other Washington units, has been extremely diffused. McIntyre carried the ball in reducing the federal deficit from $38 to $30 billion. "Dr. No." has gained much respect from the Washington establishment but "finds himself at the helm of OMB when the institutional influence of the once-powerful budget agency has been declining."[12]

OMB can live with its reputation so long as distinctions are maintained between the President's need for a politically sensitive OMB *and* the President's utilization of OMB as a partisan instrument for managing the executive branch. OMB can serve a President in many ways, but it is unparalleled for offering an analytic and reasonably impartial perspective on Executive Branch programs. A President who believes he no longer needs an institutional conscience loses what the OMB exists to provide. OMB must play within the game rules if it is to survive as a credible presidential staff. A President has many people telling him what to do, but he needs a staff which can perform the essential support functions effectively. So long as it is that "abominable no-man," OMB can take the heat as an occupational hazard. Recent experience has revealed, however, that an Office of Meddling and Bumbling gains little credibility in the executive establishment and helps neither itself nor the President.

OMB's future as a presidential staff office will be determined not by machinery per se, but by the quality of leadership and direction from the President. The OMB is still the closest thing a President has to an interest-free perspective on Executive Branch policies, but only if the President distinguishes institutional from personal staff services. As Dale McOmber of OMB recently reported, "there's not a lot of difference under Mr. Carter. We've got a lot of knowledge here and the people in the White House are in a search for knowledge, knowledge of what's happening in the Government and how they can get to the mechanisms that make it run. OMB is in a position to provide that kind of knowledge."[13] OMB's recent problems stemmed not from arbitrary usurpation of power or loss of credibility, but from the misuse of OMB for purposes which had neither credibility nor validity. A lesson to all Presidents should be that OMB staff at all levels can be engaged in policymaking as well as coordination—so long as it is performed without the spur of preordained partisan program decisions that set forth what, when, how, and by whom. It is otherwise impossible to make or coordinate policy—or to be objective. No OMB can protect the President and develop options when White House staff interpose themselves and their judgments between staff agency and President. The more things change, the more they remain the same.

Appendices
Bibliography
References

List of Directors
Office of Management and Budget

Charles G. Dawes
June 23, 1921 to June 30, 1922

Herbert M. Lord
July 1, 1922 to May 31, 1929

J. Clawson Roop
August 15, 1929 to March 3, 1933

Lewis W. Douglas
March 7, 1933 to August 31, 1934

Daniel W. Bell
September 1, 1934 to April 14, 1939

Harold D. Smith
April 15, 1939 to June 19, 1946

James E. Webb
July 31, 1946 to January 27, 1949

Frank Pace, Jr.
February 1, 1949 to April 12, 1950

Frederick J. Lawton
April 13, 1950 to January 21, 1953

Joseph M. Dodge
January 22, 1953 to April 15, 1954

Rowland R. Hughes
April 16, 1954 to April 1, 1956

Appendices

Percival F. Brundage
  April 2, 1956 to March 17, 1958

Maurice H. Stans
  March 18, 1958 to January 21, 1961

David E. Bell
  January 21, 1961 to December 20, 1962

Kermit Gordon
  December 28, 1962 to June 1, 1965

Charles L. Schultze
  June 1, 1965 to January 28, 1968

Charles J. Zwick
  January 29, 1968 to January 21, 1969

Robert P. Mayo
  January 22, 1969 to June 30, 1970

George P. Shultz
  July 1, 1970 to June 11, 1972

Caspar W. Weinberger
  June 12, 1972 to February 1, 1973

Roy L. Ash
  February 2, 1973 to February 3, 1975

James T. Lynn
  February 5, 1975 to January 21, 1976

Thomas B. Lance
  January 22, 1977 to September 21, 1977

James T. McIntyre
  March 24, 1978 to Present

Organization Charts of BOB/OMB

Appendices

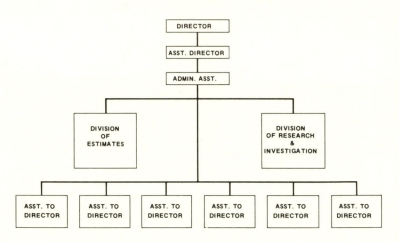

A. 1921-1938

DIRECTOR

ASST. DIRECTOR

ADMIN. ASST.

DIVISION OF ESTIMATES

DIVISION OF RESEARCH & INVESTIGATION

ASST. TO DIRECTOR

ASST. TO DIRECTOR

ASST. TO DIRECTOR

ASST. TO DIRECTOR

ASST. TO DIRECTOR

ASST. TO DIRECTOR

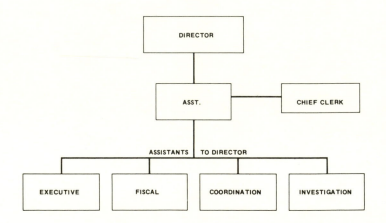

B. 1939

DIRECTOR

ASST.

CHIEF CLERK

ASSISTANTS TO DIRECTOR

EXECUTIVE

FISCAL

COORDINATION

INVESTIGATION

136

C. 1945

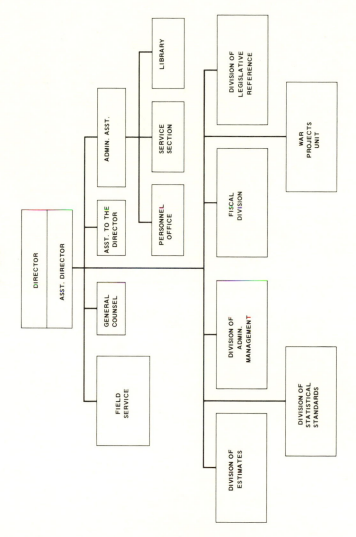

DIRECTOR

ASST. DIRECTOR

FIELD SERVICE

GENERAL COUNSEL

ASST. TO THE DIRECTOR

ADMIN. ASST.

PERSONNEL OFFICE

SERVICE SECTION

LIBRARY

DIVISION OF ESTIMATES

DIVISION OF ADMIN. MANAGEMENT

FISCAL DIVISION

DIVISION OF LEGISLATIVE REFERENCE

DIVISION OF STATISTICAL STANDARDS

WAR PROJECTS UNIT

D. 1952

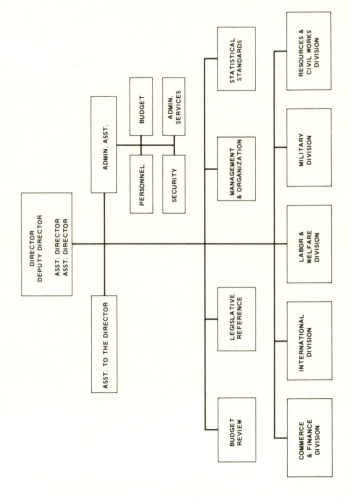

DIRECTOR
DEPUTY DIRECTOR
ASST. DIRECTOR
ASST. DIRECTOR

ASST. TO THE DIRECTOR

ADMIN. ASST.

PERSONNEL

BUDGET

SECURITY

ADMIN. SERVICES

BUDGET REVIEW

LEGISLATIVE REFERENCE

MANAGEMENT & ORGANIZATION

STATISTICAL STANDARDS

COMMERCE & FINANCE DIVISION

INTERNATIONAL DIVISION

LABOR & WELFARE DIVISION

MILITARY DIVISION

RESOURCES & CIVIL WORKS DIVISION

E. 1967

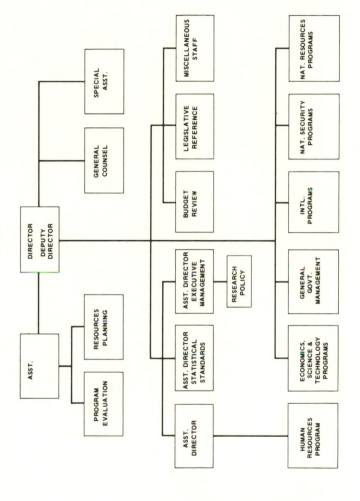

F. 1970

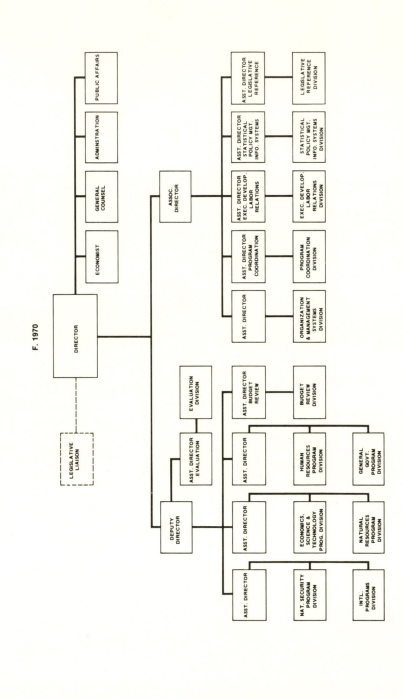

G. 1975

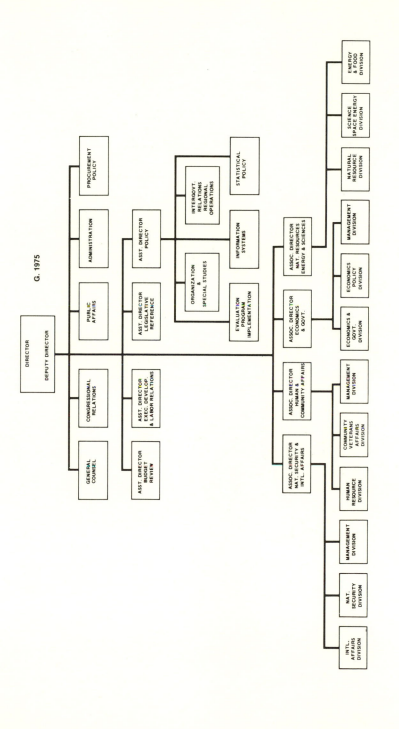

H. 1978

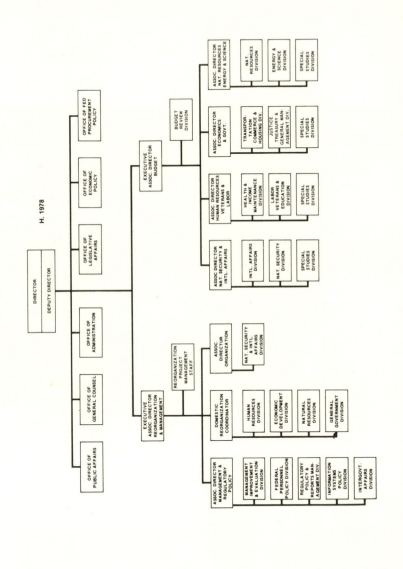

BIBLIOGRAPHY

Aberbach, J., and Rockman, B. "Clashing Beliefs Within the Executive Branch: The Nixon Administration Bureaucracy." *American Political Science Review*, 70 (June 1976), pp. 456-468.

Adams, S. *Firsthand Report*. New York: Harper and Brothers, 1961.

Appleby, P. "Harold D. Smith—Public Administrator," *Public Administration Review* 7 (Spring 1947), pp. 77-81.

Berman, L. "OMB and the Hazards of Presidential Staff Work." *Public Administration Review* 38 (Nov/Dec 1978), pp. 520-524. "The Office of Management and Budget That Almost Wasn't." *Political Science Quarterly*, 92 (Summer 1977).

Bombardier, G. "The Managerial Function of OMB: Intergovernmental Relations as a Test Case." *Public Policy*, 23 (Summer 1975), pp. 317-354.

Bonafede, D. "Carter Staff is Getting Itchy to Make the Move to Washington." *National Journal*, 8 (October 30, 1976), pp. 1542-1547.

————. "Lynn Seeks Compromise in His Role as OMB Director." *National Journal*, 7 (May 24, 1975), p. 767.

————. "Powerful OMB Reaches Adolescence." *National Journal*, 6 (June 22, 1974), pp. 932-936.

————. "The Making of the President's Budget: Politics and Influence in a New Manner." *National Journal*, 3 (January 23, 1971), pp. 151-165.

————. "Ehrlichman Acts as Policy Broker on Nixon's Formalized Domestic Council." *National Journal*, 3 (June 12, 1971), pp. 1225-1242.

The Brookings Institution. "Study of the 1960-61 Presidential Transition: The White House and the Executive Office of the President." Washington, D.C.: The Brookings Institution, 1960. Mimeographed.

Brownlow, L. *The President and the Presidency*. Chicago: Public Administration Service, 1949.

Bibliography

Brundage, P. *The Bureau of the Budget.* New York: Praeger, 1970.

――――. "The Federal Budget: Recent Trends and Future Opportunities (and Role of the Office of Management and Budget)." *Price Waterhouse Review,* 15 (Autumn 1970), pp. 6-21.

Burkhead, J. *Government Budgeting.* New York: John Wiley and Sons, Inc., 1956.

Califano, J. *A Presidential Nation.* New York: W.W. Norton and Co. Inc., 1975.

Carey, W. "Reorganization Plan No. 2." *Public Administration Review,* 30 (November-December 1970), pp. 631-634.

――――. "Presidential Staffing in the Sixties and Seventies." *Public Administration Review,* 29 (September-October 1969), pp. 450-458.

――――. "Roles of the Bureau of the Budget." *Science,* 156 (April 14, 1967), pp. 206-208.

――――. "The Roles of the Bureau of the Budget." Paper given at the Fourteenth Annual Meeting of the Markle Scholars, Lake Placid, New York, September 30, 1966.

Carter, J. "Making Government Work Better: Economic Policy-Making." *National Journal,* 8 (October 16, 1976), p. 1491.

Cleveland, F. "Evolution of the Budget Idea in the United States." *Annals of the American Academy of Political and Social Science* (November 1915).

Coffey, J. I., and Rock, V. P. *The Presidential Staff.* Washington, D.C.: National Planning Association, 1961.

Cronin, T. "Everybody Believes in Democracy Until He Gets to the White House." *Law and Contemporary Problems,* 35 (Summer 1971), pp. 573-625.

Culliton, B. "Office of Management and Budget: Skeptical View of Scientific Advice." *Science,* 183 (February 1, 1974), pp. 392-396.

Davis, J. W. and Ripley, R. B. "The Bureau of the Budget and Executive Branch Agencies." *Journal of Politics,* 29 (November 1967), pp. 749-769.

Dawes, C. G. *The First Year of the Budget of the United States.* New York: Harper and Brothers Publishers, 1923.

Derthick, M. *Between State and Nation.* Washington, D.C.: The Brookings Institution, 1974.

144

Egger, R. "The United States Bureau of the Budget." *Parliamentary Affairs*, 3 (Winter 1949), pp. 39-54.

Ehrlichman, J. "How it All Began . . . By a Man Who Was There." *National Journal*, 7 (December 13, 1975), pp. 1689-1690.

Eisenhower, D. D. *Waging Peace: 1956-1961*. Garden City, New York: Doubleday, 1965.

Emmerich, H. *Federal Organization and Administrative Management*. Alabama: The University of Alabama Press, 1971.

Fairlie, H. "Thoughts on the Presidency." *Public Interest*, 9 (Fall 1967), pp. 28-48.

Fisher, L. *Presidential Spending Power*. Princeton, N.J.: Princeton University Press, 1975.

George, A. "Assessing Presidential Character." *World Politics*, 26 (January 1974), pp. 234-282.

———. "The 'Operational Code': A Neglected Approach to the Study of Political Leaders and Decision-Making." *International Studies Quarterly*, 13 (June 1969), pp. 190-212.

Gilmour, R. "Central Legislative Clearance: A Revised Perspective." *Public Administration Review*, 31 (March-April, 1971), pp. 150-158.

Ginzberg, E., and Solow, R. *The Great Society: Lessons for the Future*. New York: Basic Books, 1974.

Gordon, G. J. "Office of Management and Budget Circular A-95: Perspectives and Implications." *Publius*, 4 (1974), pp. 45-68.

Greenberger, R., "Carter's Budget Chief," *New York Times*, November 30, 1978.

Greenstein, F., Berman, L., and Felzenberg, A. *Evolution of the Modern Presidency: A Bibliographical Survey*. Washington, D.C.: American Enterprise Institute for Public Policy Research, 1977.

Hamill, K. "This is a Bureaucrat." *Fortune*, 48 (November 1953), pp. 156-158.

Harper, E. L., Kramer, F. A., and Rouse, A. M. "Implementation and Use of PPB in Sixteen Federal Agencies." *Public Administration Review*, 29 (1969), pp. 623-632.

Havemann, J. "OMB's New Faces Retain Power, Structure Under Ford." *National Journal*, 7 (July 26, 1975), pp. 1070-1075.

―――. "Budget Reform Legislation Calls for Major Procedural Change." *National Journal*, 6 (1974), pp. 734-742.

―――. "OMB Begins Major Program to Identify and Attain Presidential Goals." *National Journal*, 5 (June 2, 1973), pp. 783-793.

―――. "OMB's Legislative Role is Growing More Powerful and More Political." *National Journal*, 5 (October 27, 1973), pp. 1589-1598.

Heclo, H. "OMB and the Presidency: The Problem of Neutral Competence." *Public Interest*, 38 (Winter 1975), pp. 80-98.

Heller, D., and Heller, D. "The Extraordinary Powers of the Bureau of the Budget." *American Legion Magazine*, 79 (August 1965), pp. 8-12.

Herbers, J. "The Other Presidency." *New York Times Magazine* (March 3, 1974), pp. 16+.

Hess, S. *Organizing the Presidency*. Washington, D.C.: The Brookings Institution, 1976.

Hobbs, E. *Behind the President: A Study of the Executive Office Agencies*. Washington, D.C.: Public Affairs Press, 1954.

Holcombe, A. N. "Over-All Financial Planning Through the Bureau of the Budget." *Public Administration Review*, 1 (Spring 1941), pp. 225-230.

Hyde, J., and Wayne, S. "Partners in Presidential Policy-Making: White House-OMB Legislative Relationships." Paper delivered at the 1975 Annual Meeting of the Southern Political Science Association, Nashville, Tennessee, November 6-8, 1975. Mimeographed.

Ickes, H. *The Secret Diary of Harold L. Ickes: The First Thousand Days, 1933-1936*. Vol. 1. New York: Simon and Schuster, 1953.

Johnson, L. B. *The Vantage Point: Perspectives of the Presidency 1963-1969*. New York: Popular Library, 1971.

Johnson, R. T. *Managing the White House: An Intimate Study of the Presidency*. New York: Harper and Row, Publishers, 1974.

Jones, R. "The Role of the Bureau of the Budget in the Federal Legislative Process." *American Bar Association Journal*, 40 (November 1954), pp. 995-998.

Karl, B. *Executive Reorganization and Reform in the New Deal:*

The Genesis of Administrative Management, 1900-1939. Cambridge: Harvard University Press, 1963.

Kearns, D. *Lyndon Johnson and the American Dream.* New York: Harper and Row, 1976.

―――. "Lyndon Johnson's Political Personality." *Political Science Quarterly,* 91 (Fall 1976), pp. 385-409.

Kessel, J. H. *The Domestic Presidency: Decision-Making in the White House.* Massachusetts: Duxbury Press, 1975.

Koenig, L. W. *The Chief Executive.* New York: Harcourt, Brace and World, 1968.

Kraft, J. "Washington. Insight: The Remarkable Mr. Gordon and His Quiet Power Center." *Harper's Magazine* (May 1965), pp. 40-50.

Latham, E. G. "Executive Management and the Federal Field Service." *Public Administration Review,* 5 (Winter 1945), pp. 16-27.

Lawton, F. J. "Legislative/Executive Relations in Budgeting as Viewed by the Executive." *Public Administration Review,* 13 (1953), pp. 169-176.

Lewis, F., and Zarb, F. "Federal Program Evaluation from the OMB Perspective." *Public Administration Review,* 34 (July-August 1974), pp. 308-317.

Maass, A. "In Accord with the Program of the President." *Public Policy,* 9 (1953), pp. 77-93.

MacMahon, A. W. "The Future Organizational Pattern of the Executive Branch," *American Political Science Review,* 38 (December 1944), pp. 1179-1191.

―――. "Congressional Oversight of Administration: The Power of the Purse." *Political Science Quarterly,* 58 (June-September 1943), pp. 407-414.

Merriam, R. E. "The Bureau of the Budget as Part of the President's Staff." *Annals of the American Academy of Political and Social Science,* 307 (September 1956), pp. 15-23.

Moe, R. C. "The Domestic Council in Perspective." *The Bureaucrat,* 5 (October 1976), pp. 251-272.

Moley, R. *After Seven Years.* New York: Harper and Brothers, 1939.

Morestein-Marx, F. *The President and His Staff Services.* Chicago, Ill.: Public Administration Service, 1947.

147

―――. "The Bureau of the Budget: Its Evolution and Present Role." *American Political Science Review*, 39 (August and October 1945), pp. 653-684 and 869-898.

Mosher, F. C., et al. *Watergate: Implications for Responsible Government*. New York: Basic Books, Inc., 1974.

Mullaney, T. R. "OMB Pushes Plans to Improve Federal Management: Still No Miracles." *National Journal*, 3 (October 4, 1971), pp. 2378-2388.

Murphy, L. V. "Organization and Major Functions of the Bureau of the Budget; Establishment, Legislative Mission, Growth of the Bureau, Functional Activity, Present Status." Washington, D.C.: Office of Management and Budget Library, 1950. Mimeographed.

Nathan, R. P. "The Administrative Presidency." *Public Interest*, 15 (Summer 1976), pp. 40-54.

―――. *The Plot That Failed: Nixon and the Administrative Presidency*. New York: John Wiley and Sons, Inc. 1975.

National Academy of Public Administration. *The President and Executive Management: Summary of Symposium*. Washington, D.C.: October 1976. Mimeographed.

―――. *Conference on the Institutional Presidency*. Preliminary Papers. Airlie House, Va., March, 1974. Mimeographed.

Neustadt, R. *Presidential Power, the Politics of Leadership With Reflections on Johnson and Nixon*. 2nd ed. New York: John Wiley and Sons, Inc., 1976.

―――. "Approaches to Staffing the Presidency: Notes on FDR and JFK." *American Political Science Review*, 57 (December 1963), pp. 855-864.

―――. "Presidency and Legislation: Planning the President's Program." *American Political Science Review*, 49 (December 1955), pp. 980-1021.

―――. "Presidency and Legislation: The Growth of Central Clearance." *American Political Science Review*, 48 (September 1954), pp. 641-671.

―――. "Presidential Clearance of Legislation: Legislative Development, Review and Coordination in the Executive Office of the President." Ph.D. dissertation, Harvard University, 1950.

Osborne, J. *The First Two Years of the Nixon Watch*. New York: Liverwright, 1971.

Pearson, N. M. "A General Administrative Staff to Aid the President." *Public Administration Review,* 4 (Spring 1944), pp. 127-147.

————. "The Budget Bureau: From Routine Business to General Staff." *Public Administration Review,* 3 (Spring 1943), pp. 126-149.

————. "The Budget in Federal Administrative Management." Ph.D. dissertation, University of Chicago, 1943.

Pennock, J. R. "Responsiveness, Responsibility, and Majority Rule," *American Political Science Review,* 46 (September 1952), pp. 790-807.

Polenberg, R. *Reorganizing Roosevelt's Government, 1936-1939.* Cambridge: Harvard University Press, 1966.

Pressman, J. and Wildavsky, A. *Implementation: How Great Expectations in Washington are Dashed in Oakland; Or, Why It's Amazing That Federal Programs Work at All, This Being a Saga of the Economic Development Administration as Told by Two Sympathetic Observers Who Seek to Build Morals on a Foundation of Ruined Hopes.* Berkeley: University of California Press, 1973.

Price, D. K. "General Dawes and Executive Staff Work." *Public Administration Review,* 10 (Summer 1951), pp. 167-172.

Ramsey, J. W. "The Director of the Bureau of the Budget as a Presidential Aide, 1921-1952; with Emphasis on the Truman Years." Ph.D. dissertation, The University of Missouri, 1967.

Rappaport, P. "The Bureau of the Budget: A View From the Inside." *Journal of Accountancy,* 101 (March 1956), pp. 31-37.

Reese, J. H. "The Role of the Bureau of the Budget in the Legislative Process." *Journal of Public Law,* 15 (January 1966), pp. 63-93.

Rose, R. *Managing Presidential Objectives.* New York: The Free Press, 1976.

Roth, H. "The Executive Office of the President: A Study of its Development with Emphasis on the Period 1939-1953." Ph.D. dissertation, Washington: The American University, 1958.

Samuelson, R. J. "The People Everyone Loves to Hate." *Washingtonian,* 11 (November 1975), pp. 62-90.

Schell, J. *The Time of Illusion.* New York: Alfred Knopf, 1976.

Schick, A. "The Taking of OMB: The Office of Management

149

and Budget During the Nixon Years." Paper delivered at Princeton University Conference on Advising the President, October 31, 1975. Mimeographed.

———. "A Death in the Bureaucracy: The Demise of Federal PPB." *Public Administration Review*, 33 (March-April 1973), pp. 146-156.

———. "The Budget Bureau That Was: Thoughts on the Rise, Decline, and Future of a Presidential Agency." *Law and Contemporary Problems*, 35 (Summer 1970), pp. 519-539.

———. "PPB's First Years: Premature and Maturing." Washington, D.C.: The Brookings Institution, 1968. Mimeographed.

———. "The Road to PPB: The Stages of Budget Reform." *Public Administration Review*, 26 (December 1966), pp. 243-258.

Schlesinger, A. M. *A Thousand Days: John F. Kennedy in the White House*. Boston: Houghton Mifflin Co., 1965.

Schuck, V. "Anatomy of Change: Reorganization Plan No. 2 of 1970." Festschrift for Karl Loewenstein, *J.C.B. Mohr (Paul Siebeck) Tubingen*, 1971, pp. 391-425.

Seckler-Hudson, C., ed. *Budgeting: An Instrument of Planning and Management*. Washington, D.C.: Department of Public Administration, School of Social Sciences, American University, 1944-1945.

Seidman, H. *Politics, Position and Power: The Dynamics of Federal Organization*. New York: Oxford University Press, 1975.

Shantz, M. L. "The Division of Administrative Management of the Bureau of the Budget, 1939-1952." Washington, D.C. OMB Library. Mimeographed.

Sharkansky, I. *Public Administration: Policy Making in Government Agencies*. Chicago: Markham, 1970.

Smith, H. D. *The Management of Your Government*. New York: McGraw Hill, 1945.

———. "The Budget as an Instrument of Legislative Control and Executive Management." *Public Administration Review*, 4 (Summer 1944), pp. 131-188.

———. "The Bureau of the Budget." *Public Administration Review*, 1 (Winter 1941), pp. 106-115.

Somers, H. M. *Presidential Agency OWMR: The Office of War*

Mobilization and Reconversion. Cambridge, Mass.: Harvard University Press, 1950; reprinted ed., New York: Greenwood Press, 1969.

Sorensen, T. C. *Kennedy.* New York: Bantam Books, 1965.

Stafford, S. " 'Political' OMB Cuts Agencies to Size." *Government Executive,* 7 (August 1974), pp. 48-53.

Stans, M. "The President's Budget and the Role of the Bureau of the Budget." *Federal Accountant,* 9 (September 1959), pp. 5-16.

Stanton, N. "History and Practice of Executive Impoundment of Appropriated Funds." *Nebraska Law Review,* 53 (1974), pp. 1-30.

Stein, H., ed. *Public Administration and Policy Development.* New York: Harcourt, Brace and Co., 1952.

Sundquist, J. *Making Federalism Work.* Washington, D.C.: The Brookings Institution, 1969.

Thomas, N., and Wolman, H. "The Presidency and Policy Formulation: The Task Force Device." *Public Administration Review,* 29 (September-October 1969), pp. 454-470.

U.S. Executive Office of the President, Bureau of the Budget. *The Bureau of the Budget During the Administration of Lyndon B. Johnson.* 2 Vols. November 14, 1968. Washington, D.C.: OMB Library. Mimeographed.

———. *The Work of the Steering Group Evaluation of the Bureau of the Budget.* 3 Vols. February-July, 1967. Washington, D.C.: OMB Library. Mimeographed.

———. *The Bureau of the Budget—What Is It—What It Does.* Washington, D.C.: Government Printing Office, 1966.

———. *Staff Orientation Manual.* Washington, D.C.: Government Printing Office, 1945, 1963.

———. *The United States at War.* Washington, D.C.: Government Printing Office, 1946.

U.S. National Archives. *Federal Records of World War II, Vol. 1 Civilian Agencies.* Washington, D.C.: Government Printing Office, 1950.

U.S. President's Committee on Administrative Management. *Report of the Committee with Studies of Administrative Management in the Federal Government.* Washington, D.C.: Government Printing Office, 1937.

Wade, L. L. "The U.S. Bureau of the Budget as Agency Evalu-

151

ator: Orientation to Action." *American Journal of Economics and Sociology*, 27 (January 1968), pp. 55-62.

————. "Decision-Making in the U.S. Bureau of the Budget with Special Reference to the Divisions of Labor-Welfare and Resources-Civil Works." Ph.D. dissertation, University of Oregon, 1965.

Waldman, R. J. "The Domestic Council: Innovation in Presidential Government." *Public Administration Review*, 36 (1976), pp. 260-268.

Walsh, J. "Office of Management and Budget: New Accent on the 'M' in OMB." *Science*, 183 (January 25, 1974), pp. 286-290.

————. "Office of Management and Budget: The View From the Executive Office." *Science*, 183 (January 18, 1974), pp. 180-182.

Wann, A. J. "Franklin D. Roosevelt and the Bureau of the Budget." *Business and Government Review*, 9 (March-April 1968), pp. 32-41.

Wayne, S. *The Legislative Presidency*. New York: Harper and Row, 1978.

Wayne, S., and Hyde, J. "Presidential Decision-Making: The Politics of the Enrolled Bill Process." Paper delivered at the 1975 Annual Meeting of the American Political Science Association, San Francisco, California. September 2-5, 1975. Mimeographed.

Wildavsky, A. *The Politics of the Budgetary Process*, 2nd ed. Boston: Little, Brown, 1974.

————. *Dixon-Yates: A Study in Power Politics*. New Haven: Yale University Press, 1962.

Wilkie, H. "Legal Basis for Increased Activity of the Federal Budget Bureau." *George Washington Law Review*, 11 (April 1943), pp. 265-301.

Williams, J. D. "The Impounding of Funds by the Bureau of the Budget." The Inter-University Case Program, Cases in Public Administration and Policy Formation: #28, Syracuse University, 1955.

Willoughby, W. F. *The Problem of a National Budget*. New York: Appleton, 1918.

Wood, R. "When Government Works." *The Public Interest*, 18 (Winter 1970), pp. 39-51.

REFERENCES

PREFACE

1. William Carey, "Reorganization Plan No. 2," *PAR* 30 (November/December, 1970), p. 634.

2. Henry Fairlie, "Thoughts on the Presidency," *The Public Interest* 9 (Fall 1967), p. 36. Even though no comprehensive account of BOB/OMB exists, there are several important writings on the years through 1979. See Charles Dawes, *The First Year of the Budget of the United States* (New York: Harper and Brothers, 1923); Harold Smith, "The Bureau of the Budget," *PAR* 1 (Winter 1941), pp. 106-115; Norman Pearson, "The Budget Bureau: From Routine Business to General Staff," *PAR* (Spring 1943), pp. 126-149; *Ibid.* "A General Administrative Staff to Aid the President," *PAR* 4 (Spring 1944), pp. 127-147; Horace Wilkie, "Legal Basis for Increased Activity of the Federal Budget Bureau," *GW Law Review* 11 (April 1943), pp. 265-301; Fritz Morstein Marx, "The Bureau of the Budget: Its Evolution and Present Role," (2 Parts), *APSR* 39 (August and October 1945), pp. 653-684, 869-898; Arthur Maass, "In Accord with the Program of the President," *Public Policy* 4 (1953), pp. 77-93; Richard Neustadt, "Presidency and Legislation: The Growth of Central Clearance," *APSR* 48 (September 1954), pp. 641-671; *Ibid.* "Presidency and Legislation: Planning the President's Program" *APSR* 49 (December 1955), pp. 980-1021; Robert Merriam, "The Bureau of the Budget as Part of the President's Staff," *The Annals* 307 (September, 1956), pp. 15-23; A. J. Wann, "Franklin D. Roosevelt and the Bureau of the Budget," *Business and Government Review* 9 (March-April 1968), pp. 32-41; Larry Lee Wade, "The U.S. Bureau of the Budget as Agency Evaluator," *The American Journal of Economics and Sociology* 27 (January 1968), pp. 55-62; John Reese, "The Role of the Bureau of the Budget in the Legislative Process," *Journal of Public Law* 15 (1966), pp. 63-93; James Davis and Randall Ripley, "The Bureau of the Budget and Executive Branch Agencies: Notes and Their Interaction," *JP* 29 (Novem-

153

References

ber 1967), pp. 749-769; Allen Schick, "The Budget Bureau That Was: Thoughts on the Rise, Decline and Future of a Presidential Agency," *Law and Contemporary Problems* 35 (Summer 1970), pp. 519-520; Percival Brundage, *The Bureau of the Budget* (New York: Praeger, 1970); Robert Gilmour, "Central Legislative Clearance: A Revised Perspective," *PAR* 31 (March-April 1971), pp. 150-158; Gary Bombardier, "The Managerial Function of OMB: Intergovernmental Relations as a Test Case," *Public Policy* 23 (Summer 1975), pp. 317-354; Hugh Heclo, "OMB and the Presidency—The Problem of Neutral Competence," *The Public Interest* 38 (Winter 1975), pp. 80-98; Larry Berman, "The Office of Management and Budget That Almost Wasn't," *PSQ* 92 (Summer 1977); *Ibid.* "OMB and the Hazards of Presidential Staff Work," *PAR* 38 (November-December 1978), pp. 520-524.

CHAPTER ONE

1. Louis Fisher, *Presidential Spending Power* (New Jersey: Princeton University Press, 1975), p. 32. Fisher shows that several 19th-century Presidents actively participated in revising budget estimates.

2. U.S. Commission on Economy and Efficiency, *The Need for a National Budget* (Washington, D.C.: Government Printing Office, 1912). Commission members included Frederick Cleveland, Frank Goodnow, William Willoughby, Walter Warnick, and Merritt Chance.

3. See U.S. Congress. *A National Budget System: A Compilation of Hearings, Reports, Acts, Bills, Tracing the Legislative Development of the Budget and Accounting Act.* (2 Vols. Washington, D.C.: Government Printing Office, 1918-1921).

4. 42 Stat. 20 (1921).

5. U.S. Bureau of the Budget. *Staff Orientation Manual* (Washington, D.C.: Government Printing Office, 1945), p. 23.

6. Dawes, *The First Year of the Budget of the United States*, p. 63.

7. Don Price, "General Dawes and Executive Staff Work," *PAR* 10 (Summer 1941), p. 169.

8. Dawes, *The First Year of the Budget of the United States*, p. 178.

9. *Ibid.*, preface.

10. See Joseph Kraft, "Washington Insight: The Remarkable Mr. Gordon and His Quiet Power Center," *Harper's Magazine*, vol. 230 (May 1965), p. 40.

11. Dawes, *The First Year of the Budget of the United States*, p. 283.

12. *Staff Orientation Manual*, 1945, p. 38.

13. *Ibid.*, pp. 16-17.

14. See Harold Ickes, *The Secret Diary of Harold L. Ickes: The First Thousand Days, 1933-1936*, Vol. 1. (New York: Simon and Schuster, 1953), p. 659; Raymond Moley, *After Seven Years* (New York: Harper and Brothers, 1939), p. 166.

15. Memorandum, Lewis Douglas to President Roosevelt, December 30, 1933. Official File 79, 1933-1935. Franklin D. Roosevelt Library.

16. Memorandum, Lewis Douglas to President Roosevelt, August 30, 1934. President's Personal File 194. Franklin D. Roosevelt Library.

17. Wann, "Franklin D. Roosevelt and the Bureau of the Budget," p. 37.

18. Neustadt, "Presidency and Legislation: The Growth of Central Clearance," p. 650.

19. *Ibid.*, pp. 655-656.

20. Herbert Emmerich, *Federal Organization and Administrative Management* (University, Alabama: The University of Alabama Press, 1971), pp. 207-208. The three-man committee consisted of Chairman Louis Brownlow, Charles E. Merriam and Luther Gulick. Emmerich, a staff member of the Brownlow Committee, provided a verbatim transcript from the meeting.

21. U.S. President's Committee on Administrative Management, *Report of the Committee, with Studies of Administrative Management in the Federal Government* (Washington: Government Printing Office, 1937), p. 16.

22. *Ibid.*, p. 20.

23. *Ibid.*, p. 21.

24. *Staff Orientation Manual*, 1945, p. 40.

25. See Richard Polenberg, *Reorganizing Roosevelt's Government, 1936-1939* (Cambridge: Harvard University Press, 1965); Barry Karl, *Executive Reorganization and Reform in the New*

Deal: The Genesis of Administrative Management, 1900-1939 (Cambridge: Harvard University Press, 1963).

26. While major shifts did occur between the 1937 report and the 1939 legislation, the recommendations for the Bureau of the Budget remained mostly unchanged. See Harvey Mansfield, "Federal Executive Reorganization: Thirty Years of Experience." *PAR* 29 (July/August 1969), pp. 332-345; Harvey Mansfield, "Reorganizing the Federal Executive Branch: The Limits of Institutionalization." *Law and Contemporary Problems* 35 (Summer 1970), pp. 461-495.

CHAPTER TWO

1. Memorandum, Harold Smith to Members of the Staff, May 18, 1939. Records of the Bureau of the Budget, Records Group 51, Box B2-1. File 1939-40 Organization, Functions and Activities. Hereafter cited as *1939 Smith Poll*.

2. Memorandum, Tom Cargill to Harold Smith, May 26, 1939, *1939 Smith Poll*.

3. Memorandum, Robert Adamy to Harold Smith, May 29, 1939, *1939 Smith Poll*.

4. "Suggested Improvements in the Organization and Procedure of the Bureau of the Budget," July 24, 1939, *1939 Smith Poll*; See Harold Smith to Staff Members of the Bureau, July 24, 1939. Office Memorandum No. 5. *1939 Smith Poll*.

5. V. L. Almond to Harold Smith, May 19, 1939, *1939 Smith Poll*.

6. L. W. A'Hearn to Harold Smith, May 23, 1939, *1939 Smith Poll*. This undoubtedly reflects Roosevelt's own penchant for fostering competitiveness and overlapping assignments amongst aides.

7. *Ibid.* This undoubtedly reflected FDR's penchant for fostering competitiveness between aides.

8. "Suggested Improvements in the Organization and Procedure of the Bureau of the Budget," p. 11.

9. Memorandum, C. L. Dasher to Harold Smith, May 23, 1939, *1939 Smith Poll*.

10. Diary of Harold Smith, August 28, 1940. Franklin D. Roosevelt Library.

11. Diary of Harold Smith, July 7, 1939.

12. *Ibid.*, May 25, 1940.

13. *Ibid.*, October 2, 1939.

14. Letter, Harold Smith to J. Weldon Jones, October 20, 1939. Papers of J. Weldon Jones. Acceptance of Job File. Harry S Truman Library.

15. Letter, Edward Kemp to J. Weldon Jones, December 9, 1939. Papers of J. Weldon Jones. Acceptance of Job File. Harry S Truman Library.

16. Letter, Wayne Coy to J. Weldon Jones, June 13, 1940. Papers of J. Weldon Jones. Acceptance of Job File. Harry S Truman Library. See Daily Calendar of Harold Smith, July 3, 1940.

17. Richard Neustadt, "Roosevelt's Approach to the Budget Bureau" (Mimeo, attachment B of memorandum from Richard Neustadt to President-elect John Kennedy, October 30, 1960), p. 3.

18. Stephen Hess, *Organizing the Presidency.* (Washington, D.C. The Brookings Institution, 1965), p. 42.

19. Harold Seidman, *Politics, Position and Power: The Dynamics of Federal Organization*, 2nd ed. rev. (New York: Oxford University Press, 1975), p. 76.

20. Paul Appleby, "Harold D. Smith—Public Administrator," *Public Administration Review* 7 (Spring 1947), p. 80.

21. Diary of Harold Smith, November 2, 1943.

22. Neustadt, "Roosevelt's Approach to the Budget Bureau," p. 2.

23. Diary of Harold Smith, April 28, 1939.

24. *Ibid.*, April 25, 1939.

25. *Ibid.*, May 31, 1939.

26. *Ibid.*, June 6, 1940.

27. *Ibid.*, April 12, 1941.

28. *Ibid.*, December 4, 1942.

29. Memorandum, Harold Smith to President Roosevelt, November 23, 1942. Official File, Franklin D. Roosevelt Library; emphasis mine.

30. Diary of Harold Smith, December 30, 1939.

31. *Ibid.*, January 16, 1940.

32. *Ibid.*, January 18, 1940.

33. *Ibid.*, August 11, 1939.

34. Memorandum, President Roosevelt to Harold Smith,

References

December 9, 1944. Papers of Harold Smith, Miscellaneous. Franklin D. Roosevelt Library.

35. Transcript, Roger Jones, Oral History interview, January, 1970, p. 5. Harry S Truman Library.

36. See U.S. National Archives. *Federal Records of World War II, Vol. 1 Civilian Agencies* (Washington, D.C.: Government Printing Office, 1950), p. 90; See U.S. Bureau of the Budget, *The United States at War* (Washington, D.C.: Government Printing Office, 1946); U.S. Congress, House. Committee on Appropriations. *Independent Office Appropriation Bill for 1944.* (Washington, D.C.: Government Printing Office, 1942), p. 732.

37. Herman Somers, *Presidential Agency OWMR.* (Cambridge: Harvard University Press, 1950; reprinted ed., New York: Greenwood Press, 1969), pp. 66-70.

38. *Ibid.,* p. 67.

39. Diary of Harold Smith, January 4, 1945.

40. Memorandum, Harold Smith to President Truman, April 13, 1945. Papers of Harold Smith, Franklin D. Roosevelt Library.

41. Memorandum, Harold Smith to Bureau of the Budget Staff, April 13, 1945. Papers of Harold Smith, Franklin D. Roosevelt Library.

42. Diary of Harold Smith, April 18, 1945. See Memorandum, r.b. to Matthew Connelly, April 17, 1945. President's Official File, Harry S Truman Library.

43. *Ibid.*

44. Neustadt, "The Growth of Central Clearance," p. 658.

45. Diary of Harold Smith, April 18, 1945.

46. *Ibid.,* April 26, 1945. Emphasis mine.

47. *Ibid.*

48. Roger Jones, Letter to the author.

49. *Ibid.,* May 4, 1945.

50. Notes of Dan Biederman from an interview with Roger Jones, January 10, 1976. I am indebted to Dan Biederman for allowing me to quote from the interview transcript.

51. Diary of Harold Smith, May 4, 1945.

52. Richard Rose, *Managing Presidential Objectives* (New York: The Free Press, 1965), pp. 41-42.

158

53. Transcript, Roger Jones Oral History Interview, January 1970, p. 23. Harry S Truman Library.

54. Memorandum, Harold Smith to President Truman, October 30, 1945. Subject File. Harry S Truman Library.

55. Diary of Harold Smith, May 5, 1945. Emphasis mine.

56. *Ibid.*, August 18, 1945.

57. *Ibid.*, January 31, 1946.

58. See Harold Smith Daily Record. Telephone conversation with James Byrnes, Secretary of State, Friday, March 8, 1946; Telephone conversation between Ben Cohen, State Department, and Mr. Smith, Friday, March 15, 1946, at 11:45 a.m. #11, Franklin D. Roosevelt Library.

59. Harold Smith to President Truman, June 19, 1946. Papers of Harold Smith. Franklin D. Roosevelt Library.

60. *Ibid.*

61. Letter, President Truman to Harold Smith, June 19, 1946. President's Official File. Harry S Truman Library.

62. Neustadt, "Roosevelt's Approach to the Budget Bureau," p. 3.

63. Diary of Harold Smith, December 19, 1945.

64. Letter, Harold Smith to President Truman, June 12, 1946. Papers of Harold Smith, Franklin D. Roosevelt Library.

65. Transcript of Press Conference, July 25, 1946. *Harry S Truman, Public Papers of the Presidents of the United States, 1946.* (Washington, D.C.: Government Printing Office, 1964), p. 356.

66. Personal interview with James Webb, January 30, 1976.

67. Neustadt, "The Growth of Central Clearance," p. 657.

68. James Webb, Conference notes, August 15, 1946. Papers of James Webb, A 3-4 Conference Notes. Harry S Truman Library.

69. Transcript, Roger Jones Oral History Interview, January 1970, p. 7. Harry S Truman Library.

70. Neustadt, "Growth of Central Clearance," p. 660.

71. Clark Clifford to James Webb, January 8, 1947. Clark Clifford Collection, Box 2, Bureau of the Budget File. Harry S Truman Library.

72. Personal interview with James Webb, January 30, 1976.

73. *Ibid.*

References

74. *Ibid.*

75. Neustadt, "The Growth of Central Clearance," p. 661.

76. Transcript, Roger Jones Oral History Interview, January 1970, p. 3. Henry S Truman Library.

77. Letter, James Webb to President Truman, November 5, 1948. Papers of James Webb. Box 2 File C2-1 The President. Harry S Truman Library.

78. "Study of the 1960-61 Presidential Transition: The White House and the Executive Office of the President," Mimeographed (Washington, D.C.: Brookings Institution), pp. 12-13.

79. Hess, *Organizing the Presidency*, p. 6.

80. V. O. Key, "Draft Report on Executive Office," pp. 24-31. Records of the Bureau of the Budget, Records Group 51, E2-50/45.1.

81. See both Memorandum, Elmer Staats to James Webb, "Organization of the Bureau of the Budget," August 22, 1947. Records of the Bureau of the Budget, B2-1. OMB Records. Memorandum, Elmer Staats to James Webb, "Organization and Management of the Bureau of the Budget," September 25, 1947. Papers of Fred Lawton, Box 3, BOB Organization File. Harry S Truman Library.

82. Elmer Staats to James Webb, September 25, 1947, p. 1.

83. *Ibid.*

84. See "Staff Report on the Organization of the Bureau of the Budget," B2-1. Records of the Bureau of the Budget. Records Division OMB.

85. See "Review of the Organization of the Bureau of the Budget," June, 1951. Records of the Bureau of the Budget. Records Division OMB.

86. See Report to the Director: A Self-Study of the Bureau of the Budget," May 1, 1959. Records of the Bureau of the Budget. Records Division of OMB.

CHAPTER THREE

1. Transcript, Elmer B. Staats Oral History Interview, p. 14, July 13, 1964. John F. Kennedy Library.

2. See letter, President Eisenhower to Joseph Dodge, November 10, 1952. Whitman Collection, Box 9. Dodge File (5). Dwight D. Eisenhower Library. Letter, Joseph Dodge to Fred

Lawton, November 11, 1952. Papers of Fred Lawton, Correspondence—Official Misc. File. Harry S Truman Library.

3. Transcript, Elmer B. Staats Oral History Interview, pp. 13-14, July 13, 1964. John F. Kennedy Library.

4. Transcript, Roger Jones Oral History Interview, p. 18, July 13, 1967. Dwight D. Eisenhower Library.

5. *Ibid.*

6. Neustadt, "Planning the President's Program," p. 985.

7. *Ibid.*, p. 988.

8. *Ibid.*, p. 990.

9. *Staff Orientation Manual*, 1963, p. 21.

10. See Transcript, Roger Jones Oral History Interview, pp. 31-32, July 13, 1967. Dwight D. Eisenhower Library.

11. Personal interview with James Webb, January 30, 1975.

12. U.S. Congress, House. Committee on Appropriations. *Independent Offices Appropriations* (Washington, D.C.: Government Printing Office, 1954), p. 615.

13. Memorandum, R. M. Macy to P. Rappaport, "Review of Organization and Functions of the Bureau." February 6, 1956. Records of the Bureau of the Budget, Record Series 51, File B2-1. OMB Records Division.

14. Memorandum, William McCandless to Mr. Rappaport, "Improving Operations in the Office of Budget Review," March 2, 1956. *1956 Study*.

15. Memorandum, William Carey to P. Rappaport, "Appraisal of Bureau's Performance and Resources," February 9, 1956. *1956 Study*.

16. R. M. Macy to P. Rappaport, February 6, 1956.

17. See Memorandum, Percy Rappaport to the Director. "Survey of the Organization and Staffing of the Bureau of the Budget," April 16, 1956. *1956 Study*; "Principal Conclusions of 1956 Survey of the Bureau of the Budget," undated; "Summary of Office and Division Heads Comments in Connection with 1956 Survey of Organization and Operations of Bureau of the Budget," undated, *1956 Study*; Memorandum, The Director to Percy Rappaport. "Survey of the Organization and Staffing of the Bureau of the Budget," April 25, 1956. *1956 Study*.

18. Dwight D. Eisenhower, *Waging Peace: 1956-1961* (Garden City, New York: Doubleday, 1965), p. 385, 387.

19. Personal interview with Maurice Stans, January 8, 1976.

References

20. Memorandum, Phillip Hughes to William Carey, "Possible Criticisms of the Bureau," August 5, 1960. Records of the Bureau of the Budget, B2-1. Records Division of OMB. See Memorandum, William Carey to all Division Chiefs, "Request for List of Possible Criticisms of the Bureau," August 4, 1960. Records of the Bureau of the Budget, Records Series 51. B2-1. Records Division OMB.

21. Brookings Institution, "The White House and Executive Office," p. 18.

22. Hess, "Organizing the Presidency," p. 76.

23. "Organizing and Relating the Budget Bureau's Activities to the Sixties and Seventies," p. 19.

24. "Need for the proposed Office of Executive Management," December 23, 1958, PACGO, Box 12, Folder 71.

25. Nelson Rockefeller to President Eisenhower, January 3, 1957. "Office of Administration in the Executive Office of the President," PACGO, Box 11, File 69.

26. Notes of A. J. Goodpaster, "Memorandum of Conference with the President," January 10, 1957. Whitman Diaries, Eisenhower Library, Folder: January 1957, Diary-Staff memos.

27. *Ibid.*

28. Nelson Rockefeller to President Eisenhower, October 10, 1957. "White House-Executive Organization for Management Activities," PACGO, Box 11, File 69.

29. Percival Brundage to Governor Adams, November 18, 1957. "Executive Office Organization for Management Activities," PACGO, Box 11, File 69.

30. Arthur Kimball and Jerry Kieffer to Nelson Rockefeller, Milton Eisenhower, and Arthur Flemming, November 27, 1957. "Executive Office Organization for Management Activities," Box 11, File 69, p. 1.

31. Jerry Kieffer and John Kennedy to Dr. Milton Eisenhower, October 1, 1959. "Reorganization of Management Functions in the Executive Office of the President," PACGO, Box 12, File 71, p. 12.

32. This is a well-known dictum of public administration, named for its author, Rufus Miles, long-time HEW and BOB official and former director of the Mid-Career Program in the Woodrow Wilson School at Princeton University.

33. "A Bill to Facilitate the President's Exercise of Certain

Executive Functions: The Executive Management Act, 1958,"
April 3, 1958. (G.D.M.) PACGO, Box 11, File 70, pp. 1-2.

34. Jerry Kieffer, memorandum for the record. "Presidency-Management Functions," December 27, 1957, PACGO, Box 11, File 69.

35. Arthur Kimball to Nelson Rockefeller, Dr. Milton Eisenhower, and Dr. Arthur Flemming, April 22, 1958. "Proposed Executive Assistant to the President," PACGO, Box 11, File 70.

36. Arthur Kimball, memorandum for the record. "Meeting in Governor Adams' Office on May 8, 1958 to consider Proposed Office of Executive Management," PACGO, Box 12, File 71.

37. This information was provided by Mr. Stans in a letter to the author, September 17, 1976.

38. Kieffer and Kennedy to Milton Eisenhower, October 1, 1958.

39. *Ibid.*

40. Arthur Kimball to Nelson Rockefeller, Milton Eisenhower, and Arthur Flemming, November 28, 1958. "Executive Office Organization and Management Activities," PACGO, Box 12, File 71.

41. Robert Gray, Secretary of the Cabinet, to the Honorable Arthur Summerfield, the Postmaster General, December 11, 1958. PACGO, Box 12, File 71.

42. See "Reorganization Plan No. 1 of 1959." Draft, January 20, 1959, PACGO, Box 12, File 71.

43. Jerry Kieffer to the Secretary of the Cabinet, January 22, 1959. "Office of Executive Management," PACGO, Box 12, File 71.

44. Arthur Kimball to Milton Eisenhower, January 18, 1959. "Personal," PACGO, Box 12, File 71. On July 1, 1960, Nelson Rockefeller appeared before the Jackson Subcommittee on National Security Organization and recommended the creation of an Executive Assistant to the President *and* a Director of the Office of Executive Management "to assist in planning and management in the sphere of domestic affairs." Rockefeller's recommendation represented the culmination of PACGO's efforts to improve the management process in the EOP.

45. "Report to the Director: A Self-Study of the Bureau of the Budget," May 1, 1959. Records of the Bureau of the Budget, Records Division OMB, emphasis mine.

References

46. *Ibid.*, p. 6.

47. *Ibid.*

48. *Ibid.*, p. 95.

49. Memorandum, Members of the Study Group to Director Stans. May 1, 1959. *1959 Study*.

50. Memorandum, Maurice Stans to Members of the Bureau Staff Study Group, "Completion of Director's Review of 'Self-Study of the Bureau of the Budget.'" September 29, 1959. *1959 Study*. For a more detailed account see Berman, 1977.

51. Transcript, David Bell Oral History Interview, July 11, 1964, p. 8. John F. Kennedy Library.

CHAPTER FOUR

1. Richard Neustadt, "Memorandum on Staffing the President-elect," October 30, 1960, p. 18. Records of the Bureau of the Budget. Transition File E2-24/60. Records Division OMB.

2. Brookings Institution, "The White House and Executive Office," p. 33.

3. Transcript, Phillip Hughes Oral History Interview, April 24, 1968, p. 2. John F. Kennedy Library.

4. *Staff Orientation Manual*, 1963, p. 21.

5. Theodore Sorenson, *Kennedy* (New York: Bantam, 1965), pp. 281-325.

6. "Organizing Around the Director," p. 3.

7. Memorandum, Kermit Gordon to President Johnson, November 23, 1963. FI4 Budget-Appropriation. Lyndon Baines Johnson Library. See also a report prepared by BOB staffer John D. Young for Bill Moyers entitled "President Johnson's First 100 Days and the Bureau of the Budget." Records of the Bureau of the Budget, B2-1, November 15, 1966. Records Division OMB.

8. Memorandum, William Carey to Bill Moyers, "Spot Assistance by the Bureau of the Budget," November 26, 1963. FG11-1. Lyndon Baines Johnson Library.

9. Memorandum, Kermit Gordon to President Johnson, November 25, 1963 in Young, p. 11.

10. Young, "President Johnson's First 100 Days and the Bureau of the Budget," pp. 18-19.

164

11. Walter Heller to President Johnson, "Case for a $101-102 billion Budget," November 25, 1963. FI4, Lyndon Baines Johnson Library.

12. Memorandum, Kermit Gordon to President Johnson, November 26, 1963. FI4, Lyndon Baines Johnson Library.

13. *Ibid.*

14. Personal interview with Kermit Gordon, December 12, 1975.

15. *Public Papers*, "Remarks to Members of the Budget Bureau Staff at the Signing of the 1965 Budget, January 20, 1964. Young, Part II, p. 26.

16. Lyndon Johnson to Kermit Gordon, May 31, 1965, FG11-1. Lyndon Baines Johnson Library. In his resignation letter, Gordon noted "I want to convey my deep appreciation for your personal kindness, and for your perceptive and unwavering support of the Bureau of the Budget in its vital but largely anonymous work. . . . The career staff of the Bureau is one of the brightest ornaments of the public service. Your confidence in that staff, and your generous recognition of its work, has inspired its members to maximum effort and has rekindled its dedication to the cause for which the Bureau exists—the service of the Presidency." See Kermit Gordon to President Johnson, May 26, 1965, FG11-1. Lyndon Baines Johnson Library.

17. These books and other relevant materials are now available at the Lyndon Baines Johnson Library.

18. Transcript, James Gaither Oral History Interview, Tape #3, p. 1, January 25, 1972. Lyndon Baines Johnson Library.

19. U.S. Congress, House. *Presidential Advisory Committee.* Hearings before a Subcommittee of the Committee on Government Operations (Washington, D.C.: Government Printing Office, 1970), pp. 161-162.

20. *The Bureau of the Budget During the Administration of President Lyndon B. Johnson.* November 1963-January 1969, 2 Vols. Lyndon Baines Johnson Library, 1969, pp. 101-102. This document, an administrative history of the BOB from 1963-1969, was compiled by Bureau staff for use in the 1968 presidential transition.

21. "Roles and Missions—II," p. 23.

22. Carey, "Presidential Staffing," p. 451.

References

23. *Ibid.*

24. Personal interview with Kermit Gordon, December 12, 1975.

25. Personal interview with Charles Zwick, January 5, 1976.

26. Memorandum, Larry Levinson to George Christian, January 11, 1968. CG/Charles Schultze. Lyndon Baines Johnson Library.

27. Transcript, Matthew Nimetz Oral History Interview, January 7, 1969, p. 41. Lyndon Baines Johnson Library.

28. *Ibid.*, p. 40.

29. Memorandum, Dan Witt to James Jones, *Eyes only.* "BOB/White House Debriefing," June 1, 1965. CF/FE9. Lyndon Baines Johnson Library.

30. Carey, "Presidential Staffing in the Sixties and Seventies," p. 454.

31. Transcript, Harold Seidman Oral History Interview, April 1971, p. 5. Harry S Truman Library. Emphasis mine.

32. See Memorandum, Robert Semer to President Johnson, October 1, 1966, FG11-8-1. Lyndon Baines Johnson Library. Memorandum, Harold Seidman to Charles Schultze, "Study of Federal Grants-in-Aid," July 9, 1966. Records of the Bureau of the Budget, Records Series 51, B2-1. Records Division OMB.

33. *The Bureau of the Budget During the Administration of Lyndon Baines Johnson*, p. 127.

34. "Task Force Report on Intergovernmental Program Coordination," in *The Bureau of the Budget During the Administration of Lyndon Baines Johnson*, Vol. II.

35. *Ibid.*, emphasis mine.

36. U.S. Congress, House. Committee on Appropriations. *Treasury, Post Office and General Government* (Washington, D.C.: Government Printing Office, 1967), pp. 666-664. Emphasis mine.

37. *Ibid.*

38. "Creative Federalism: Report on Field Surveys of Problems in Administering Intergovernmental Programs," in *The Bureau of the Budget During the Administration of President Lyndon Baines Johnson*, Vol. II.

39. U.S. Congress, Senate. *Establish a Commission on the Organization and Management of the Executive Branch*, Hearings before the Subcommittee on Executive Reorganization of

the Committee on Government Operations. (Washington, D.C.: Government Printing Office, 1968), p. 2.

40. Carey, "Presidential Staffing in the Sixties and Seventies," p. 452.

41. See Charles Murphy to President Johnson, "Heineman Task Force Report," November 22, 1968, FG11-8 1969. Lyndon Baines Johnson Library. See Task Forces (1966 Outside), Box 4. "Outside 1966 Task Force on Government Organization." The papers of Fred Bohen, staff director of the Heineman Task Force, contain the official report and several working papers. Lyndon Baines Johnson Library.

42. *Heineman Report**, p. 6. A final draft of the report dated June 16, 1967 was condensed for the President's reading. The asterisk refers to the unabridged draft of the report, but is not available in the Johnson Library.

43. *Heineman Report*, p. 8.

44. *Heineman Report**, p. 10.

45. *Heineman Report*, p. 10.

46. *Ibid.*

47. *Heineman Report*, p. 9.

48. *Ibid.*, p. 8.

49. *Heineman Report**, p. 18.

50. *Ibid.*, p. 20.

51. *Heineman Report*, p. 12.

52. *Ibid.*, p. 10.

53. *Ibid.*, p. 11.

54. *Ibid.*

55. Allen Schick, "Some Budgetary Prerequisites for Program Planning: A Critical Analysis," p. 19. Bohen Papers. Lyndon Baines Johnson Library. Cf. Rufus Miles, "Some Observations on the President's Problem of Managing the Executive Branch" (Paper prepared for the President's Task Force on Government Organization, April 7, 1967). Miles argued that an Office of Policy Studies should be established in the White House.

56. *Heineman Report**, p. 25.

57. Memorandum, John McCarter to Phillip Hughes, "A Plan for a Study of the Bureau," February 7, 1967, in "The Work of the Steering Group on Evaluation of the Bureau of the Budget" (February-July 1967), 3 Vols. (unpublished manuscript in the Library of the Office of Management and Budget).

167

References

58. *Ibid.*

59. Memorandum, Charles Schultze to Office and Division Chiefs, "Evaluation of the Organization and Management of the Bureau of the Budget," February 24, 1967. The Steering Group consisted of Director Schultze, Deputy Director Sam Hughes, Assistant Directors Carey, Zwick and Hoffman, and Special Assistant to the Director Roger Jones. Outside members included Kermit Gordon, Dwight Ink, Harry McPherson, Rufus Miles, Wallace Sayre, Charles Stauffacher, and Sydney Stein.

60. "Minutes of Meeting," March 25, 1967. *The Work of the Steering Group.* See "Working Paper and Related Analysis on Roles and Missions of the Bureau of the Budget—I," March 30, 1967. Pp. 7-8.

61. "Minutes of Meeting," March 25, 1967, p. 8.

62. "Roles and Missions—I," p. 2.

63. *Ibid.*, p. 15.

64. *Ibid.*, pp. 8-9.

65. "Organizing Around the Director," p. 10.

66. "Roles and Missions—I," p. 15; see Minutes of March 25, 1967 meeting.

67. *Ibid.*, p. 14.

68. *Ibid.*

69. *Ibid.*, p. 15.

70. "Organizing Around the Director," pp. 2-3. Emphasis mine.

71. "Organizing and Relating the Budget Bureau's Activities in the Sixties and Seventies," May 19, 1967, pp. 15-16.

72. "Bureau of the Budget: A Composite of External Views," p. 3.

73. "Organizing and Relating the Budget Bureau's Activities to the Sixties and Seventies," p. 19.

74. "The High Level Personnel Problem in the Bureau of the Budget," Administratively Confidential, p. 1.

75. Merrill J. Collett, "The Management of Professional Staff in the Bureau of the Budget," June 1967, pp. 4-5.

76. *Ibid.*, pp. 11, 44. The report noted that contrary to widespread opinion, "the professional work force of the Bureau is highly immobile."

77. *Ibid.*

78. "The High Level Personnel Problem," p. 1.

79. *Ibid.*, pp. 2-3.

80. *Ibid.*, p. 3.

81. Schick, "The Budget Bureau That Was," p. 532.

82. *Ibid.*

83. "Organizing Around the Director," p. 5.

84. *Ibid.*, p. 11.

85. Memorandum, Joseph Califano to President Johnson, March 11, 1967. FG 749/Exec. Box 406. Lyndon Baines Johnson Library.

86. "An Orderly Approach to Achieving Change in the Management and Organization of the Bureau of the Budget," June 15, 1967, p. 5.

87. Memorandum, Charles Schultze to President Johnson, "Reorganization of the Budget Bureau," July 22, 1967. Records of the Bureau of the Budget. Records Series 51, B2-1. Records Division OMB.

88. Seidman, *Politics, Position and Power*, p. 85.

89. Maass, "In Accord With the Program of the President," p. 82.

90. Seidman, p. 211.

91. Carey, "Presidential Staffing in the Sixties and Seventies," p. 451.

92. Carey, "Reorganization Plan No. 2," p. 631.

93. "Roles and Missions," pp. 7-8.

94. Bombardier, "The Managerial Function of OMB," p. 324.

CHAPTER FIVE

1. Cited in memorandum, Roy Ash to President Nixon, "The Executive Office of the President," August 20, 1969, p. 2.

2. In Ash's transition memo, the DPC was located within a larger OEM. To obtain John Ehrlichman's support for the reorganization plan, however, the DPC was moved outside the OEM and given an independent reporting relationship to Ehrlichman and the White House.

3. Memorandum, Roy Ash to President Nixon, August 20, 1969, p. 2. Argued that the "structure of the Executive Office pervasively influences the effectiveness of the entire Executive Branch."

4. Memorandum, Roy Ash to President Nixon, "Proposed

Organization of the Executive Office of the President," October 17, 1969, p. 3.

5. Memorandum, Roy Ash to President Nixon, October 17, 1969, p. 8.

6. *Ibid.*, p. 18.

7. See Weekly Compilation of Presidential Documents, March 16, 1970 (Washington, D.C.: Government Printing Office, 1970), pp. 355-357.

8. Interview with Roy Ash, November 6, 1975. See Berman, "The OMB That Almost Wasn't."

9. Information provided to the author by Richard Tanner Johnson, senior staff associate of the Ash Council. Johnson kept verbatim transcripts of all Council meetings and a diary of the Council's work.

10. These issues were raised by Mayo in a December 16, 1969 letter to Roy Ash.

11. Information supplied to the author by Richard Tanner Johnson.

12. *Ibid.*

13. *Ibid.*

14. U.S. Congress, Senate, Subcommittee on Executive Reorganization and Government Research, Committee on Government Operations, *Hearings on Reorganization Plan No. 2 of 1970*, 91st Congress, 2nd Session, May 7, 1970, p. 31.

15. *Ibid.*, p. 35.

16. *Ibid.*, p. 35. Emphasis mine.

17. Heclo, "OMB and the Presidency," p. 91.

18. Schick, "The Budget Bureau That Was," p. 520.

19. Carey, "Reorganization Plan No. 2," p. 631.

20. Interview with Roy Ash, November 6, 1975.

21. OMB Press Release, Friday August 7, 1970. Records of the Bureau of the Budget, B2-1 (1970). Records Division OMB. Emphasis mine.

22. "The Office of Management and Budget's New Role—An External View." (Panel No. 3, Federal Management Improvement Conference, October 19, 1971), p. 2. Records of the Office of Management and Budget. B2-1/1971. Records Division OMB.

23. *Ibid.*, p. 10.

24. "The President and Executive Management: Summary of

a Symposium," (The National Academy of Public Administration, 1976), p. 19. Mimeographed.

25. *Ibid.*, p. 20.

26. Dom Bonafede, "The Making of the President's Budget: Politics and Influence in a New Manner," *National Journal* 3 (January 23, 1971), p. 151.

27. John Osborne, *The First Two Years of the Nixon Watch* (New York: Liverwright, 1971), p. 107. In testimony before the House Judiciary Committee in 1973, Alexander Butterfield (an aide to Haldeman) recounted that in a typical year, 72 percent of President Nixon's time was spent with H. R. Haldeman, 10 percent with Henry Kissinger, and 8 percent with John Ehrlichman. This left only 4-5 percent for Ron Ziegler and "others." Butterfield included among these "others" OMB Director George Shultz (July 1, 1970-June 11, 1972), and Shultz saw more of President Nixon than any of the President's other Budget Directors (Robert Mayo, Casper Weinberger, and Roy Ash). See U.S. Congress, House. *Impeachment of Richard M. Nixon, President of the United States, Report of the Committee on the Judiciary* (Washington, D.C.: Government Printing Office, 1974).

28. Remarks by Roger Jones, "Conference on the Institutional Presidency" (Preliminary Papers, National Academy of Public Administration, March, 1974), p. 52.

29. Notes from Biederman interview with Roger Jones, January 10, 1975.

30. See Joel Havemann, "OMB's Legislative Role is Growing More Powerful and More Political," *National Journal* 5 (October 27, 1973), pp. 1589-1598.

31. "The President and Executive Management," p. 18.

32. Fisher, *Presidential Spending Power*, p. 56.

33. Stephan Wayne, Richard Cole, and James Hyde, Jr., "Advising the President on Legislation: Patterns of Executive Branch Influence," (Paper presented at the 1977 Annual Meeting of the American Political Science Association), pp. 9, 12.

34. "The Senate Watergate Report," *The Final Report of the Senate Select Committee on Presidential Campaign Activities* (New York: Dell Books, 1974), p. 332.

35. "A Self-Study of the Bureau of the Budget," May 1, 1959, p. 107.

36. "A Composite of External Views," p. 17.

References

37. *Ibid.*

38. Aaron Wildavsky, *The Politics of the Budgetary Process*, 2nd ed. (Boston: Little, Brown, 1974), p. xviii.

39. John Herbers, "The Other Presidency," *New York Times Magazine*, March 3, 1974, p. 16.

40. Richard Nathan, "The Administrative Presidency," *Public Interest* 44 (Summer 1976), p. 76.

41. Personal interview with Roy Ash, November 6, 1975.

42. Joel Havemann, "OMB's New Faces Retain Power, Structure Under Ford," *National Journal* 7 (July 26, 1975), p. 1074.

43. Personal interview with Roy Ash, November 6, 1975.

44. U.S. Congress, House. Subcommittee of the Committee on Government Operations, *Confirmation of the Director and Deputy Director of the Office of Management and Budget* (Washington, D.C.: Government Printing Office, 1973).

45. Carey, "Reorganization Plan No. 2," p. 631.

46. Memorandum, Roy Ash to General Haig, May 25, 1973, p. 4. Director's File 7502-5. Records of the Office of Management and Budget. Records Division OMB.

47. Heclo, "OMB and the Presidency," p. 90.

48. Frederick Mosher, et al. *Watergate: Implications for Responsible Government* (New York: Basic Books, 1974), pp. 41-42.

CHAPTER SIX

1. Heclo, "OMB and the Presidency," p. 84.

2. *Ibid.*, p. 88.

3. These transition recommendations are cited in U.S. Congress, Senate. *Nominations of Thomas B. Lance and James T. McIntyre, Jr.* (Washington, D.C.: Government Printing Office, 1977), p. 40.

4. Philip Shabecoff, "Budget Office Withstands Moves to Cut its Power," *New York Times* (November 11, 1974).

5. "The President and Executive Management," p. 18.

6. See U.S. Congress, Senate. Hearings before the Committee on Government Operations, *Nomination of James T. Lynn* (Washington, D.C.: Government Printing Office, 1975). Louis Fisher noted that "the lack of preparation by committee members and their staff was painfully obvious. From the desultory

questioning it appeared that the committee was discharging an unwanted, embarrassing task. No one in the room would have known that the hearings constituted an act of congressional reassertion." Fisher, *Presidential Spending Power*, pp. 54-55.

7. Joel Havemann, "OMB's New Faces Retain Power, Structure Under Ford," *National Journal* 7 (July 26, 1975), p. 1074.

8. Jimmy Carter, "Making Government Work Better: Economic Policy-Making," *National Journal*, 8 (October 16, 1976), p. 1491.

9. U.S. Congress, House. *Reorganization Plan No. 1 of 1977* (Washington, D.C.: Government Printing Office, 1977), p. 49.

10. *Nominations of Thomas B. Lance and James T. McIntyre, Jr.*, p. 42.

11. Personal Interview with Bert Lance, November 16, 1977.

12. Robert Greenberger, "Carter's Budget Chief." *New York Times*, November 30, 1978. In addition, two recent developments have hampered OMB's ability to function as a general staff agency. The creation of the Office of Federal Procurement Policy in OMB, and the increasing number of statutes which limit OMB's traditional budget review role.

13. Edward Cowan, "Budget Office, While Guarding the Federal Purse, Also Plays a Key Role on Major Policy Issues," *New York Times* (January 23, 1978), p. A, 13.

INDEX

Library of Congress Cataloging in Publication Data

Berman, Larry.
  The Office of Management and Budget and the
Presidency 1921-1979.

  Bibliography: p.
  Includes index.
  1. United States. Office of Management and
Budget.   2. Presidents—United States.
I. Title.
JK421.B37   353.007'1   79-83977
ISBN 0-691-07619-7
ISBN 0-691-02197-X pbk.